W/D ✓

Saving Eagle Mitch

WITHDRAWN
From Toronto Public Library

D1366698

Contents

gallery of photos follows page 62

CONTENTS

Introduction

In my book *Feathers of Hope*, I wrote about my lifelong history of failed bird rescues, and how I wished that someday I would actually save an injured bird.

In light of that, perhaps this book should be called *Be Careful What You Wish For*, because right after *Feathers of Hope* was published, I was plunged into an international rescue attempt for a bird named Eagle Mitch from Afghanistan. This endeavor presented difficulties I never imagined, and throughout the saga I knew I had as little chance of succeeding as I had with any other bird that fell into my field of vision. But when you make certain wishes, the universe doesn't hand you what you want on a platter. It only offers yet another chance to try for it. And try I did.

For 137 days I was mired in bureaucratic red tape, writing furious rants for the press and social networks, rattling government cages I didn't know existed before, learning how to tap the power of media and politics in a whole new way. All this, for a bird.

But this was no ordinary bird, and no ordinary rescue.

Eagle Mitch was shot in Afghanistan and rescued by U.S. troops there, who continued to care for him and wanted our help to bring him safely home. He was a wild creature, regal and feisty rather than cuddly and cute, and he would never be tamed, but none of us wanted him tamed. His very being was an example of what it meant for a wild thing to survive war with dignity, with his soul intact. He was a living reminder of the best in us all, and the servicemen and -women who cared for him wanted him saved. That was a call I couldn't refuse.

Still, for me, the rescue took place during a year of great personal upheaval, mirrored in the larger political upheaval all Americans faced.

Oil was spewing into the Gulf of Mexico because of corporate greed and incompetence. Thousands of people were losing jobs and homes and pensions through the malfeasance of corporations and investment bankers, who continued to collect their six-figure bonuses and go to luxurious spas on company money. And I was engaged in a series of personal battles with institutions ranging from the Department of Motor Vehicles and Social Security to my mother's nursing home and my husband's place of employment.

Everywhere I looked, the world seemed entirely composed of mammoth, omnipotent corporate and government interests, none of which were amenable to the needs of ordinary people like you or me.

As I fought for Eagle Mitch, I rode a roller coaster of small successes that were always followed immediately by massive failures. Wending my way through federal offices, automated phone protocols, endless paperwork, and the vagaries of media interest, I grew increasingly frightened at systems that had ceased to make any human sense to me.

In spite of that, I continued to hold out hope for getting this job done. After all, a Navy SEAL was taking the trouble to care for a bird in Afghanistan, no easy task. Certainly my efforts were nothing compared to his, or those of the former Army Ranger who saved him, or the army veterinarian who took such trouble for him.

And besides, I'd gotten my stubborn on.

I would prove that humans could behave decently and sensibly. I would prove that these systems were actually capable of responding to human needs. In the process, I'd find out if I could rescue just one bird, get just one good deed done.

With my head down and my horns out, along with two fine young men and a fine young woman in uniform, I was determined to see if it was possible to bring the eagle home.

CHAPTER 1

Addle the Eggs

United States Department of the Interior
Fish and Wildlife Service

Certified Mail: 7007-0220-0002-2300-0294
Mr. Peter Dubacher
April 7, 2010

Mr. Dubacher:
    This letter is in response to your letter dated March 19, 2010 . . . reporting the laying of an eagle egg and to advise you that the authorities of the Eagle Exhibition permit MB818303 does not allow propagation; therefore, you must addle all eggs laid by the eagles in your care. . . .
    The .U.S. Fish and Wildlife Service (Service) delisted the bald eagle under the Endangered Species Act in 2007. . . . Since (on a nationwide basis), the bald eagle has recovered from the threat of extinction . . . there is no longer a need to propagate eagles.
    . . . It is your responsibility to ensure that the eagles kept under your stewardship do not reproduce. . . . Continued reproduction may result in the loss of some or all of the privileges of your permit.

April of 2010 was a busy month for both good and ill, in places both near and far from my home in upstate New York. In world news, environmental disaster dominated, most evident in the BP oil spill. On April twentieth, the BP/Transocean drilling rig Deepwater Horizon exploded in the Gulf of Mexico, killing eleven people. A blowout preventer, intended to stop the release of crude oil, failed to activate, and the waters of the Gulf started filling up with poison at a rate of approximately 250,000 gallons of oil per day.

By the end of April, wildlife experts were predicting disaster for the coast of Louisiana, which has about 40 percent of the country's wetlands. The brown pelican, recently taken off the endangered list, along with many other birds at the height of their breeding and nesting season, were at risk. Disaster was also anticipated for Louisiana's fishing industry, and this in a state that had not yet recovered from Hurricane Katrina.

While this catastrophe was playing out, two quieter events occurred in two separate parts of the world.

In upstate New York, local news carried a story about Berkshire Bird Paradise, a bird sanctuary run by Pete Dubacher. Here two permanently injured Bald Eagles, Victoria and Baldwin, were raising their newly hatched chicks. Their story was newsworthy not just because Pete's sanctuary is one of the few places where captive, injured eagles feel safe enough to lay eggs and raise young, but also because Victoria is a survivor of the Exxon Valdez oil spill. And Pete Dubacher had a lot to say about how oil spills impact birds, how important it is for humans to care for the wildlife that end up as our collateral damage.

However, the news didn't cover one aspect of the story: Pete had been ordered by the U.S. Fish and Wildlife Service to destroy Victoria's eggs. As required, he'd reported Victoria's two eggs to that office in March. He has about a dozen eagles, both golden and bald, and they've raised chicks before so he knows the routine. Then, in April, a few weeks before the BP oil spill, he received a letter from Fish and Wildlife demanding that he addle—i.e., destroy—Victoria's eggs, or his licenses would be at risk.

For a while he was afraid. First, it was way too late to destroy the eggs, since they'd already hatched, and second, he just couldn't bring himself to do it, not after a lifetime of keeping birds alive. But soon his fear turned into anger. For thirty-five years he'd invested his life in caring for birds of all kinds, a vocation he was called to by his innate kindness.

He started this work when he was in the army, serving in Panama during the Vietnam War era. While there he saw wild birds for sale in the city markets. He felt sorry for the birds, and for the people who earned a meager living by selling them. In true Pete Dubacher style, his solution was to buy the birds and set them free. When he came home, his compassion for birds continued and he started Berkshire Bird Paradise.

This calling certainly wasn't ever going to make him rich. He hadn't had a vacation in more than fifteen years, and his work was truly 24/7. But it was and is his passion, and many people have benefited from it. Thousands of schoolchildren learn about birds each year by visiting his facility. Kids in juvenile detention centers and youth-at-risk programs have their lives changed through the inspiration Pete and his work provide. He's released many eagle chicks into the wild and has saved countless birds of all kinds, giving them permanent haven whether or not they came with a donation attached.

Now a federal office was threatening him because he was successful at breeding the eagle, our national symbol of freedom and strength.

To my mind, his anger was an appropriate response. Fish and Wildlife should be sending him chocolate and flowers rather than scolding letters. And the reason they gave for the letter—that Bald Eagles aren't on the endangered list anymore—left me stammering for appropriate words.

But what bothered me most was the dehumanization the letter represented. I would guess the official who signed it knew nothing about Pete or the daily functioning of Berkshire Bird Paradise. They'd never met any of the children whose eyes grew wide with wonder when they see a mother eagle feeding her chick, children who will go on to feel a more personal investment in caring for the land and its creatures because of this experience. They were just following the rules.

Fortunately, Peter Nye, of the New York State Department of Environmental Conservation (DEC), intervened. He'd worked with Pete for a long time, and had reason to know the value of the sanctuary. He told Fish and Wildlife that New York State did want the eagles. In fact, Nye ended up bringing another eagle chick to the sanctuary, one that had been thrown from its nest during a storm. That chick was raised with Victoria and Baldwin's two. All three were later banded and released. Pete gave a sigh of relief and went back to his work.

While this small drama was enacted in upstate New York, a different story was spinning itself in the arid, open land near Kabul, Afghanistan, about 6,700 miles away. There, a young man named Scott Hickman was involved with a most unusual bird venture.

A former Army Ranger, Scott had returned to Afghanistan to work when the crashing economy took his job away. In early April, when he was training a group of Afghan soldiers, an interpreter found him and told him an eagle had been shot in the wing at a nearby shooting range. Later, he would learn that an Afghan soldier who was supposed to be using blanks had gotten some live ammunition, took a shot at the bird, and hit it.

Scott, who had an inherent interest in wildlife, went with the interpreter to see the bird. As he walked from his base camp toward the open land of the firing range part of him hoped to find the eagle dead rather than suffering. In the middle of Afghanistan, with limited resources and his time taken up by his job, he didn't know how he could help an injured bird.

Instead what he saw was an eagle lying on the ground, his wing bloodied. He tried to fly away but couldn't get more than a few yards without collapsing again. Scott approached, and the eagle's raptor eyes stared at him.

Within that primal gaze Scott saw frustration, bewilderment, and terror. The bird knew something was wrong, but he couldn't figure out why he was stuck on the ground, frozen in pain. And as all creatures do instinctively, he felt death creeping closer.

Scott bent down to him, and his compassion for the suffering he saw overrode any consideration of convenience, any question of what was possible or not possible. He had to do something to help.

He went back to his vehicle and got a sweatshirt, took it to the bird and wrapped him in it to keep him still, and brought him to help.

April 2010 was a busy month for both intelligent compassion and short-sighted greed. In ways large and small, both played themselves out, offering examples of humans at their best and their worst.

The months ahead would continue to do the same.

CHAPTER 2

Slow and Deliberate

Scott Hickman's Journal—Day 3

0730 I woke up early and attempted to feed the eagle. I pulled it out of the cage using a flat piece of stiff cardboard that I had placed the bird on as a litter. I had cut about 5–6 pieces of chicken to the size of a nickel and placed them on a paper towel. I sat on a couch and placed the bird directly across from me on a separate chair. It was lying down on its stomach and did not attempt to move but looked intently at me as if it were preparing to defend itself with escape if necessary.

All of my movements were slow and deliberate as I opened a water bottle and poured a little water onto the pieces of raw chicken. Using a pair of small needle nose pliers that were extra narrow, I proceeded to pick up a piece of chicken. I then slowly brought it to the front of the bird's face and it reacted by opening its mouth in a defensive posture. I tried touching the top of its beak with the meat and moved it close to its nostrils so that it could smell it. I then proceeded to pry a bit into the bird's mouth and forcefully put the meat onto the top of its tongue. It reacted by keeping its mouth open and staring at me with the chicken resting on its tongue. I then used the pliers to push it further into the throat down past the tongue at which point it looked like it attempted to swallow it.

After Scott wrapped his wounded eagle in a sweatshirt, he brought him back to his vehicle. He had enough experience with horses and wildlife to know that if the bird's eyes were covered he would be calmer, and if the bird was immobilized he wouldn't hurt himself more, so Scott also grabbed some electrical tape and wrapped the sweatshirt down to keep the bird still. Once he was at base camp, he put the bird in a box and brought him to a medic, just another casualty of war.

Medics do all kinds of strange things during war, but I'd have liked to see the expression on this one's face when Scott approached.

"Got a gunshot wound," Scott might have said.

The medic, looking Scott over and seeing no blood, would scratch his head. Then Scott would show him the eagle.

Okay. A war victim of a different kind.

Fortunately, the medic knew that an army veterinarian was at camp, and she had some experience with birds. Scott took his burden to her, and together they examined the wound. The bird had been shot through the wing, about an inch from the right wing joint. They couldn't pin it, but they anesthetized the bird, and went to work. They did their best to hold the fractured joint and bones in place as they worked, and when they were done they immobilized his wings, put him in a dog kennel, and brought him back to Scott's office, a relatively warm and quiet place, to see if he would live.

If there is a god of birds, or an angel specifically assigned to play guardian to their small and seemingly inconsequential lives, they couldn't have picked a better person to find Eagle Mitch than Scott Hickman. Acting on informed instinct, he did everything right each step of the way. Where others might have erred by seeing this creature through the lens of human needs, Scott—like Pete Dubacher—understood that he had to operate according to the wilder prerogatives of the avian world.

He didn't fuss over his find, but kept him warm and quiet in a place where there was minimal traffic. He covered the kennel to keep it as dark as possible, then proceeded to find the necessary resources for food.

"I never did this before," he told me, "and I was worried be-cause I wanted to get it right, though part of me already thought it was pretty hopeless."

Like me, he had a childhood riddled with failed bird rescue attempts, and he didn't want to face another one. "It feels pretty bad when that happens," he said. "But it wasn't about me. It was about this bird."

And so, he continued to mount the attempt. Like any good Army Ranger, one with experience serving in both Iraq and Afghani-stan, he was also very resourceful. He found a local source of live chickens to feed the bird, and he scoured the Internet for information on rehabilitating injured raptors. That led him to a place in Vancou-ver called Pacific Northwest Raptors, and a woman named Gill who told him how to get food and drink into the bird, also giving him a rough timetable for recovery. She told him how to "crop tube" the bird in case it wouldn't take water, since raptors get much of their liquids through their prey and this one wouldn't be able to hunt. The next day he convened with the camp medic and created a tube to get liquid into his patient.

As April bled into May, to Scott's surprise the eagle continued his recovery. Soon enough Scott was using forceps to get chicken down his throat, giving him antibiotics to ward off possible infection, and wondering what would happen next. He found that the eagle, left on his own, would manage to get himself upright, and would become agitated if too many people were around. In short time, he would actually try to escape when Scott took him out of his cage, hopping away into some corner of the tent.

As Scott wrote in his journal:

> I am waiting for it to realize that its attempts are feeble and there is no escape, sad in a way. I am actually surprised at how quickly it gets around; it kind of hops along like a robin does when searching for worms in the grass. . . . Tonight I held its feet together with my left hand and it sort of re-mained balanced in my hand as I fed with my right. We are working on coming up with plans to build it a more

permanent home which we will probably put together in the next few weeks. We will attempt to insulate it for the cold weather in the winter, we will need to come up with a way to keep it warm artificially.

Scott did build a cage, making sure to have appropriate perches and enough space and warmth for his new charge. He knew the bird would need a place to get away from human observation, a place to hide, so he made sure he had that as well.

When it became clear that the bird would live, at least for now, Scott did a very human thing and gave him a name. Mitch, he called him, after a Burmese python featured in a raucous college comedy film called *Road Trip*.

I've taught college for many years, and I recognize fine young men when I see them. Scott, and his friend Greg Wright who would later step in to help, are all that. They're also just regular young men, the kind of guys who name an eagle after a snake that attacks a nerd in a buddy comedy. The kind of guys who get together to play poker, or take their ATVs out on the sands of Afghanistan's desert to stir up some dust. So, I wondered, what impelled them to go to all this trouble?

Scott told me it was partly a lifelong attraction to raptors. He always loved hawks, loved watching them circle the skies when he was growing up in the big sky country of Wyoming. He went to school for wildlife management, and his dream was to get a job as a game warden because he loved interacting with both wildlife and people, trying to manage the interaction. He was very specific about that: it's not control but management that he went for.

But game warden jobs are hard to come by, and he and his wife found it necessary for him to take a contract position in Afghanistan. Again, like Pete Dubacher in Vietnam, at least some of his time there was spent observing the local wildlife. Before Eagle Mitch, he would observe groups of eagles soaring high above him in the clear blue sky, sometimes joining with flocks of buzzards in search of carrion, in search of the scarce food available in an arid land.

When Mitch came along Scott attached himself to the task at first mostly out of curiosity. "How often do you get to be with a raptor up close?" he said. "But then, once I saw the shape he was in, I really felt for him." His compassionate side took over, he said, a part of him that has its origins in the way he was raised.

Scott is the son of a pastor, raised in a family that was none too well-off, but one that encouraged strong ethics, a strong moral sense. Others in his community provided good examples of what that looked like as well. He remembers their own local game warden, who would take the confiscated deer from poachers and bring them to the families that needed them most. His family was fed by that game warden, and Scott hasn't forgotten that. "I didn't want to be the one who goes out and does the wrong thing," he said. "I want to be like that game warden—the one who makes wrong things right."

Of course, he continued to be a realist. It would be hard not to after serving in Iraq and Afghanistan. There were times when he was out on patrol and he'd come across a bombed-out building and find a dog with a litter of puppies. Sometimes he'd know there was nothing he could do. That's just the way it was. With Mitch, he had a chance, and he took it.

As Mitch's recovery continued and his wings were untaped, Scott interacted with him in new ways, and continued to be smart about his care. He observed early on that Mitch didn't like to be watched while he ate, so he would put the food in Mitch's cage—often a live chicken—and then walk away. One day, he turned back and saw that Mitch wasn't going after his food but instead went to the recently closed door and worked at it with his talon. He knew that was the way out, and was trying to use it. "I was amazed at how smart he was," Scott said. "He figured that one out so quick."

Though Scott had taken courses in ornithology and knew about the strength of raptors' talons, he was still astonished at what that meant in reality. When he got ready to handle Mitch he wore thick leather gloves, but the first time he let Mitch latch on, he realized there was no way to prepare for the feeling of a raptor's talon on his hand. Mitch could easily break his hand, he thought. Scott might be the caretaker, but that talon equalized the relationship, showing him the continuing strength inherent in even a wounded raptor's grasp.

When Mitch recovered enough to be allowed walks outside his cage, he would look up toward the sky, peering into what looked like endless blue. In a while, Scott would see other eagles circling close enough to be seen by the human eye—eagles Mitch had seen long before Scott did.

It's hard not to wonder if Mitch missed his bird buddies, if he instinctively yearned to be with them again, airborne, but during his exercise periods it soon became clear that Eagle Mitch would never fly again. He would make the attempt, flapping around, but his wing was broken for good. He would only get short hops off the ground from now on. Eventually, he'd have to find a permanent safe home, because he would never survive on his own in the wild.

Navy SEAL Greg Wright, Scott's ATV-riding and poker-playing friend, came into the picture then. He knew about Mitch, as did all the guys at camp, but he was thinking ahead, wondering what would happen when they all returned home in a few months.

"Hey, man, what'll you do with this eagle when we leave?" he asked Scott.

Scott wasn't sure, so Greg offered to help find Mitch a home, either in Afghanistan or in the United States. The two of them, both resourceful, intelligent young men, went about seeking a permanent home for their ward.

They tried contacting Fish and Wildlife, and got no response. An Internet search led them to a woman in England who kept birds, but she was only interested in falcons for breeding, not in injured eagles. They made inquiries about the Kabul Zoo, and what they heard about it curled the hair on the back of their necks. A zoo in a war zone was not a safe place to leave a wounded eagle.

But Greg's mom had a friend in New York who knew about a place that took birds. Maybe, she suggested, they would help. Anything, Scott said. Anything other than leaving Mitch behind.

She gave them the name Berkshire Bird Paradise, and Greg did a Google search on it, finding only good reports. So he sent an e-mail

to that bird sanctuary, more than 6,700 miles away, and through the
strange synchronicities of time, place, and event, got in touch with
the one man just crazy enough to try and help.

CHAPTER 3

Can You Help?

Subject: Possible Golden Eagle Rescue from Afghanistan
Date: Sat, 19 Jun 2010 02:19:22 -0400

I am active duty military on deployment in Afghanistan. The reason I am writing you concerns an injured Golden Eagle that our camp has in our possession that I fear will be killed soon unless rescued.

The eagle was shot by an Afghan soldier at a range. He apparently had one bullet left in his rifle and he decided to take a shot at it, and unfortunately hit it in its wing. We (the Americans on this camp) took it in and nursed it back to health, but I don't think it will fly again. When we let it out of the cage we built for him, he tries to fly, but cannot get off the ground.

Its living conditions are the best we could do with what we have, but not great. I fear that if it is not rescued out of this place, it will not live much longer. We redeploy back to the states in about 3 months and I doubt that the crew relieving us will put the effort into caring for it.

Can you help?
Thank you.
Greg Wright

The phone rang as soon as I got back from a radio interview for my book about Berkshire Bird Paradise, *Feathers of Hope*. On the other end was Pete Dubacher.

"Yes, hello, Barbara. How are you? Listen, I've got some news. I just spoke with Susan—you know, Rolf's wife? They do the e-mails and the website, and they got something real interesting," he said, talking at his usual rapid rate.

Whenever you talk to Pete, you have the sense he's listening with one ear to the many hundreds of birds in residence at his sanctuary, in case one of them needs him. And of course, he is. He's also one of the few people I know who doesn't do e-mail and has little or nothing to do with computers at all. His website and e-mail needs are all fielded by volunteers, who phone him with any important messages. I knew about Rolf and Sue, who ran his website, and I knew Pete always had something interesting going on at the sanctuary.

"What is it?" I asked.

"We got an e-mail from this guy—a Navy SEAL in Afghanistan. They saw an eagle get shot, and they've been taking care of it. It can't fly anymore, and they want to send it to us. You gotta see this e-mail. These guys—they built a cage for the bird, and they've been feeding him, and they're afraid it'll die if they don't get it somewhere safe."

He read the e-mail to me, and the one sentence "I fear that if it is not rescued out of this place, it will not live much longer" lodged itself firmly in the vicinity of my heart. My writer's mind went to work, imagining these young men in a war zone, surrounded by desert dust and the smell of gunfire, rescuing a bird. My own lifelong history of failed rescues gave me an immediate and visceral sense of the emotions involved in caring for a wounded bird, the connection that develops between you and a creature you've taken into your care.

"Wow. We have to help them," I said, without hesitation.

Pete, for his part, had a sense of history repeating itself. He was a veteran who started his bird rescue while in service. Here was another generation of soldiers rescuing birds, and they needed his help.

"Oh, yeah. You bet," he replied. "But here's the thing. They don't know how to get it here."

Yes. The thing. There's always a thing. "Then we'll figure it out," I said. "I mean, it's paperwork, right? Fish and Wildlife? Then, transportation."

"Sure. But y'know, it might be kinda hard. There's regulations and all."

"I'm sure we'll come up with something," I said confidently. "Have Sue forward the e-mail to me, and I'll take care of it."

"That'd be great," Pete said. "Thanks so much."

"No problem," I replied.

When I hung up the phone, I had no idea that I wouldn't be saying that phrase again for the duration of this mission. At the time, it seemed only right and good in an essential way to help these young men, and I anticipated a few phone calls, some irritating paperwork, maybe a newspaper campaign to help with transport costs, and a pay-off in good feelings for all concerned. In fact, it seemed like the easiest problem I had to deal with in a long time.

June was the continuation of a very difficult year for me and my family. Earlier that month, my husband Steve lost his job, suddenly, through bad politics, and we were both still reeling from the blow. Steve is very task-oriented, very committed to his work, and a man of great integrity. That, of course, means he's often a pain, insisting on everything being done right to the letter, but it also means he's incredibly trustworthy and he gets things done at work. He'd never lost a job in his life, and he'd garnered millions of dollars in grant money for this organization, so the injustice was clear, and quite shocking to us, both emotionally and financially.

We'd spoken with lawyers to see what, if anything, we could do to at least address the injustice. Repeatedly we were told that the answer was "nothing at all." No matter that the organization showed no evidence against him, the CEO had absolute control. That's because New York is a "work at will" state. Middle management, those without a contract or a union, can be booted out at the whimsy of upper management if they don't like the color of your tie. Legally, you don't have a leg to stand on.

I would be starting a new job in July, but it wouldn't pay as much as my husband's did, so we'd have to make up the difference—in an economy made stagnant by the same kind of CEOs who fired my husband. We were, to put it mildly, under some stress.

The stress was all the more pressing because it landed on shoulders made fragile by grief. In December, my mother had died, after ten months in a nursing home where my siblings and I witnessed her dementia and physical decline on a daily basis. In contrast to what was behind and around me, a straightforward bird rescue was pretty appealing.

As soon as I received my copy of the e-mail, I replied, telling Navy SEAL Greg Wright who I was. I thanked him for his compassion and told him we would be working on it.

"Don't worry," I wrote. "Pete will gladly take this bird. Do you have any thoughts on transport out of Afghanistan? If not, we'll work on that."

Greg quickly got back to me and said he could get the bird to Kabul International Airport if we could take it from there. He also told me he e-mailed Fish and Wildlife for guidance, but since they never replied he didn't know what regulations applied, or what paperwork was involved. Could we help with that, too?

Sure, I said. Of course. But as I said it, I asked myself another question. Did I know what I was doing?

The answer: not at all. In fact, I'm a paperwork disaster waiting to happen and always have been. When I was a graduate student, I failed to file my taxes for a few years, and when the IRS called to collect the money they assumed I owed them, I laughed.

"You don't get it," I told them. "You guys owe me money. I just didn't file because I'm a total idiot about forms."

That was and still is the truth. If there's anything to get wrong on an official form, I'll get it wrong. If there's any way to unwittingly offend or irritate a public official, that's what I invariably do.

However, Greg and Scott went out of their way to do the right thing. To help them, I would even face the horrors of the paperwork game, and hope to God I didn't mess it up too badly. But I'd had some important run-ins with institutions over the past year that taught me a few things about dealing with large and unwieldy systems. I had some vital lessons under my belt that would serve me well.

Nothing happens in a vacuum. Certainly in the saga of Eagle Mitch, loosely woven events, all seemingly unrelated co-occurences, conspired in a way that would do Jung's theory of synchronicity proud. Though it may seem strange, many of those threads were woven primarily through my mother's illness and death.

CHAPTER 4

I Found the Culprit

From: Nancy Wojtasek
To: Barbara Chepaitis
Subject: I think I found the culprit

Hi Barbara,

I was looking at your [astrological] chart, and I think Pluto is causing all this trouble. It's right on your ascendant, the front door to your life, basically.

Pluto's about big changes, dramatic, but works s-l-o-w-l-y. He'll come out through POWER PLAYS, and either you use the power or it'll use you. You have to learn the difference between what you can control and what you can't. Cuz, Pluto is stronger than the human will or what you want. He forces changes. Period.

Pluto transits have big power plays with institutions, companies. You have to let them know you won't take their crap, if it's just one word you utter. And Pluto is old, old stuff clearing out. When it's done, you're purified. Like going through trials of fire or initiation.

Anyways, I was just thinking about that. Most people have donuts and coffee in the morning--I think about Pluto.

Take care,
Nancy

One of the appeals of any wildlife interaction, and particularly a rescue, is that the rules are transparent, and what's necessary is straightforward. Wounds must be healed. Food and shelter must be provided. If all goes well, the creature you've rescued will survive. That can provide blessed relief from dealing with the more arbitrary and unfathomable rules of the human world, where issues of power and control, hidden agendas and complex systems come into play.

As my friend Nancy pointed out, I'd been grappling with those rules for some time. I'd known Nancy since I was a little girl. She and I and my sister Norma were an inseparable threesome throughout our grade school and high school years. When she moved to Arizona and learned astrology, we stayed in touch and she regularly sent me updates on what was going on with my stars. Whatever you think of that kind of thing, she's never once been wrong, and her insights have always been helpful.

The power issues she described, which culminated in the Eagle Mitch rescue, started the year before, when my mother broke her hip. That accident and the subsequent surgery she required greatly worsened the mild dementia she'd been coping with, and she needed full-time nursing home care. Throughout the ten months of her stay in the nursing home my siblings and I were very involved in her care, one of the five of us visiting her almost every day. And it was a good thing we were paying attention.

The first nursing home she was in had repeated issues with lack of staffing and lack of care. At one point they failed to regulate her blood thinner, and she ended up in the emergency room, bleeding uncontrollably. On some days we found her wandering unattended in her wheelchair, rummaging through charts behind the nurses' station.

She was, like Eagle Mitch, a frail and still feisty bird, injured in everything except her wild soul. Concerned for both her safety and her penchant for getting into trouble, we asked about bringing hospice in to provide extra monitoring, but the nursing home administrators discouraged us, saying, "Hospice doesn't really do much." They recommended we hire our own private duty aide for her instead, paying for it out of pocket since it wouldn't be covered by insurance.

We were considering doing that when we learned the nursing home would have to give hospice 5 percent of our mother's money if they came in, and their motives for preferring that we hire an aide suddenly made an awful kind of sense. Part of me didn't want to believe that a facility entrusted with the care of our mothers and fathers, grandmothers and grandfathers, would behave so badly, but the evidence was pretty clear. We reported the nursing home to the Attorney General, and moved our mother to a county facility with a very caring staff and a soothing resident kitty. Consistent care and comfort, a haven for the wounded, was really all she needed, and she got it there.

If my mother's illness was a stark lesson in disillusionment, what happened after her death became a primer for what I'd need to do to help Eagle Mitch. She died on December fourth, surrounded by her family and a staff that truly cared. Her funeral was held on December eleventh, which happens to be my birthday. Not exactly how I'd choose to celebrate it, but there seemed something oddly fitting in the timing. She brought me in, and I saw her out, a natural closing of a circle.

It was also natural that my mind wasn't on paperwork details, so I failed to notice that my driver's license was due for renewal the same day. I thought that wouldn't be much of a problem. Maybe I'd have to pay a fine, at worst. But when I went to the Department of Motor Vehicles to take care of it I was told I couldn't renew because there was a hold on my license.

"Because I'm late?" I asked, pretty shocked at the notion.

"No," the young woman behind the glass shield told me. "It's from OFI."

"What's that?"

"Office of Fraud Investigation."

That didn't sound good. Of course, I'd been focusing on my mother for the last ten months so maybe I'd overlooked something, but a quick memory scan of my year didn't bring any fraudulent behavior to mind. The clerks made some phone calls and found out the hold was because of a discrepancy on my Social Security card.

"What's that got to do with my license?" I asked. "And how's that fraud?"

"DMV and Social Security are connected now," the clerk told me. "Through the Patriot Act. We have to investigate everything."

I held my tongue on that one. Instead, I told her I didn't have a card. I'd had one in college, but had lost it long ago. I hadn't seen the thing in more than thirty years.

The clerks gave me the phone number of a man named Bill at OFI and told me to call him to figure it out. A brief conversation with him revealed that we had mutual friends and knew each other through a college association, so he felt assured I was actually who I purported to be. And the problem?

"Your card," he said, "has an error. Your birthdate is wrong by one number."

"That's all?" I said. That seemed simple. A typo made more than thirty years ago by a nameless clerk who had long since retired. A small problem. So, fix it.

"Can't be fixed," he said. "You'll have to go to Social Security and get a new card. Meantime, I'll let DMV know you're good to go with us."

In a weird foreshadowing of what I would soon face with Eagle Mitch, I thought this was an irritating but simple task. And I was wrong.

When I went to the Social Security office, they told me I couldn't get a new card because my license had expired. And of course DMV couldn't renew my license until I had a new card.

Anyone who ever stood in line with a peculiar problem at either of these offices will understand that the next few months were a specific kind of hell. I spent hours trying to speak to someone at Social Security, more hours trying to get DMV to give me a license. One day I made my way through the endless automated voice instructions at Social Security to an actual human, only to be put immediately on hold. Forty minutes later, the line went dead. I thought of C. S. Lewis, who imagined hell as a bureaucracy. And I began to take it personally.

My husband was sympathetic and helpful. "Why're you trying to do this on your own?" he asked. "Call your representative. They've got staff for just this kind of thing. And we pay their salaries."

That idea had never occurred to me. An American citizen all my life, I had no idea a representative could, well, represent you. At least not in such an immediate and personal way. But an Internet search on Paul Tonko—my congressional representative—yielded a phone number, so I called it.

That turned out to be the right thing to do. Tonko's constituent liaison, Domenica, quickly got through to a case manager at Social Security I'll call Sue. Domenica facilitated a three-way phone call, first begging me to hold my temper in check. I behaved.

Sue, crisp and formal, told me I had to bring in evidence of identity for a review board to look over. I gathered together my birth certificate, last year's tax forms, a recent pay stub from New York State (which had Social Security withdrawn from it, of course), an official ID from a college I'd worked at the previous semester, a letter from that same college saying they had approved my identity, and more.

I went to the Social Security office and handed it all over, chatting with Sue, keeping it deliberately positive and cheerful. But she was not so cheerful. In fact, she reminded me of my fourth grade teacher, Sister Margaret Paul, a woman who would stare grimly at her misbehaving class and pronounce coldly, "That is neither nice nor necessary."

Sue took my papers just as grimly. "It doesn't look good," she told me.

"What?" I asked.

"Your pay stubs are from last semester, and that means your photo ID might not count."

"Yeah, but I'll be working for them again in another month," I pointed out.

"That doesn't count," she said. "It doesn't prove who you are."

I stared at her, my life feeling more and more like an Escher drawing. "But you know I am who I say I am, don't you?" I asked.

She bristled. "It doesn't matter what I know. All that matters are the rules."

Personally, I've always had problems with that attitude, and sometimes I spit back something like, "That's what the Nazis said." This time I kept my mouth shut. She held my identity hostage. I'd just handed her the ransom and had to wait to see if it was enough. Clearly the power was in her hands.

About a week later, she called me. The review board didn't accept my paperwork as proof of my identity.

"But it's my taxes," I protested. "My birth certificate. My pay stub."

"It wasn't adequate," Sue told me.

"Well, can I go talk to them? Maybe that will help."

"Oh, no," she said, aghast at the notion. "They don't talk to people. They just do paper."

I thought of my mother's first nursing home, which valued its budget above the people it cared for. I thought of her second nursing home, which was much less modern in its decor, and ever so much more human in its care. I bit my lip and maintained composure. "Then what?" I asked.

"Well," she mulled, "do you have a Price Chopper Advantage card?" For those who don't know, that's the little plastic card that gets you discounts at our regional supermarket chain. There's no name or photo on it, so I was a little confused.

"Sure," I said. "Why?"

"That might establish your identity. And a cable bill could help."

Of course, I thought. This is America. I shop, and watch TV, therefore I am American. I couldn't help it—I laughed.

"I really can't recommend anything else," Sue bristled. I composed myself and told her I would come up with something.

When I got off the phone I was still feeling surreal, so I went to my computer and did something random. I looked up the date of my mother's death. All this trouble was, in some sense, because of her, and I wanted to see if there was anything about that date to guide me.

Oddly enough, there was. My mother, buried on my birthday, had died on the Feast of St. Barbara. And she had often told me she chose my name because St. Barbara was the closest saint to my birthdate.

When I read that, I shivered. The names our mothers give us are our first identity, their first gift to us. My identity was now lost in a morass of clerical errors and regulations because my mother died on the date she named me for. It felt like a bizarre combination of ghostly and governmental identity theft. But in any issue involving the government and my mother, I knew who had the upper hand.

"Mom," I muttered to her, "what are you up to?"

She had been a teacher all her life, so was she trying to give me one last lesson? If so, what did she want me to learn? All I could come up with was that with her death, it was time for me to name myself. I had to retrieve my own identity, pulling back the parts of myself I lost with her death, from the darkness of my grief.

And so I did.

I thought about the arguments I'd had with my mother about being a writer. She wanted something easier for me, something more stable. In one of our last coherent conversations she asked me if I didn't regret all the jobs I'd turned down so I could keep writing.

"No, Mom," I said. "Not at all."

She sighed. "No. I suppose not. You'd have been miserable. And I *guess* you'll be okay."

I reached over and touched her hand. "I will," I told her. "Because I was raised well." It was an important moment between us. A moment where she named her fears, and where I named myself. I started there.

That night I made photocopies of the jackets of my published novels, with my photo on them. I would put that first in my next identity packet for Social Security. Then I wrote a letter to the review board expressing my dismay at how much time and effort was being wasted on this problem. I mentioned that I was getting help from Paul Tonko and a prominent local lawyer. And I included further proof of my identity—documents naming who I truly am.

Besides the jackets from my novels, I included my marriage certificate and my son's birth certificate, and the title to our land and house. This, I thought, is who I am. A writer. A mother. Someone who loves the land. Someone who loves her husband. A citizen of this country, this state, and this county.

I handed it all in the following day, and for once I felt sure of myself, certain I had named the truth. At nine the next morning, Sue called to tell me the review board had accepted my proof. They agreed that I was who I said I was. Apparently, I just had to say who I really was.

Though I didn't realize it at the time, this would become a model of what I would need to do to rescue an eagle from Afghanistan. First and foremost, as the protagonist in my science fiction novels says, see who you are, and be what you see. Behave authentically, or stay home. Second, never take the first "no" as a final answer, especially where institutions are concerned. Finally, if you need help, call your representative.

Because of these lessons, in late June, when I was mulling how to get an eagle from Afghanistan to upstate New York, I knew to start with some political help. My only question was which politician to call. I put it to my husband.

"For this, you need a Senator," he said. "Go for Schumer. He'll have the biggest office, and the most people to deal with it."

Feeling like an old hand at dealing with politicians, I made the call to Senator Charles Schumer's New York City office with a confidence that turned out to be justified. A very pleasant young man listened to my message and pretty quickly put me through to constituent liaison Caroline Wekselbaum, whose main interests were veterans and the environment. For her, this was the perfect storm.

"How can I help you?" she asked, and I explained again about Eagle Mitch, about the young men in uniform who wanted to save him, and how we had the best possible location for him but weren't sure how to get him there. It was a speech I would repeat many times, one I would soon know by heart

"Oh, how sweet!" she said warmly. "That's so kind of them. So what exactly do you think you need?"

I appreciated her warmth and willingness to help. She understood what this would mean to two young men in a war zone and took it on wholeheartedly. She and the senator would, in fact, turn out to be our greatest support in this effort, the place I'd go to on an almost daily basis for advice. Her calm and positive attitude would become a constant source of reassurance and reason.

"Probably help with paperwork, and maybe help with transport," I said tentatively. I had never done this before, so I wasn't sure myself.

"I'll get in touch with Fish and Wildlife," she told me. "They'll respond more quickly if it comes from this office. And for transport— see if the guys can arrange anything through the military. If not, we'll figure something out."

When I got off the phone, I felt even more confident. All that mess with Social Security had paid off. I had learned how to manage this kind of thing, and I was in good hands now. I took a moment to send a whispered thanks to my mother. "You taught me well," I said. "Oddly, but well."

I e-mailed Greg and Scott, letting them know we had help and were moving forward. I was optimistic enough that I asked if they had any thoughts on transport, because it should be a matter of a week or two before we got the eagle here.

After all, it was just paperwork, and who wouldn't want to help these young men in uniform, especially since they went through so much trouble to do something so kind?

Right?

Right?

CHAPTER 5

Out of Luck

To: Wekselbaum, Caroline (Schumer)
Sent: Monday, Jun 28
Subject: Possible Golden Eagle Rescue

Dear Caroline,
   . . . I don't think there is a way to do this. The Bald and
Golden Eagle Protection Act is very restrictive and import
of live birds is prohibited in regulations 50 CFR 22.12: "You
may not transport into or out of the United States any live
bald or golden eagle . . ."
   I think they are out of luck.

Chief, Division of Management Authority
U.S. Fish and Wildlife Service

While I waited to hear back from Caroline about Eagle Mitch's permit, I chatted back and forth with Scott and Greg via e-mail. Do you
need anything, I asked them. No, we're good, they answered. We've
got everything we need.

I tried to imagine what that meant in Afghanistan, and couldn't.
Certainly they were without some very fundamental things I took for
granted, such as a peaceful existence. The sound of too many hunters
in the woods during the month of November made me nervous, and

that was nothing compared to what they dealt with. They had food, but they couldn't go to the store for a bag of Milano chocolate cookies or ice cream if they had a craving. They were far from family and home, and dealt with the possibility of violence and death on a daily basis.

Later they would both tell me that two of the most important lessons of their time in Afghanistan were not to take anything for granted, and to appreciate the richness of their lives back home.

"Kids here don't even know what a water balloon is," Scott would say. "They don't have toys."

Greg would tell me about all the wild dogs near his base. "They're not wolves or anything. Just regular dogs that are wild. I think they survive by eating human excrement. We've got Porta Johns on the range, but a lot of the locals prefer just to use the ditches, so I think that's what the dogs eat." There were so many of these dogs, he said, that it wasn't unusual for one of them to run out in front of their trucks and get hit.

I compared this with my two labs, happy creatures who anticipate treats at every turn, and usually get them. I thought about the old cars my husband and I drive, and how we didn't have to worry about driving them over IEDs on our way to the supermarket. That made me more grateful, but it didn't make me any more patient with regulations that seemed both arbitrary and inflexible.

When Caroline called to tell me that Fish and Wildlife said we couldn't bring Eagle Mitch in because it was against regulations to "import" Golden or Bald Eagles, I didn't take it well. She forwarded their e-mail to me, and my rather terse reply was that this wasn't an import. It was a rescue. But Fish and Wildlife doesn't have a rubric for "rescue." The word didn't exist in their world. That was a possibility I never considered.

My response wasn't particularly mature. I stomped around the house cursing prolifically, scaring my dogs and making my husband look up from the unemployment forms he was struggling with—another piece of bureaucratic hell we had to field.

"This organization," I growled at him, "is supposed to *protect* wild things. In April they told Pete to destroy his eagle eggs, and now they're telling me they'll stop us from helping these guys rescue an eagle that was shot. I mean, *shot*. In a war zone."

My husband rolled his eyes at me. "Yeah," he said. "What'll you do about it?"

Good question. "Something," I said. "Something *loud*."

"The dogs need a walk," he noted. "Maybe you could start there."

He knows me well. That was just what I needed. I took the dogs for an off-leash walk in the woods surrounding our house, and as they contemplated a myriad of good sniffs, I cooled down enough to think. Quickly I realized I needed either a way around the regulations or a way to shift them. I decided to try for both at once, and thought of a few places to start.

First, I e-mailed some people I know from the Mohawk Nation. Indigenous people have a different set of rules regarding their relationship to eagles, and since they're actually sovereign nations we might be able to work through them. At the least, they might be able to bring some pressure to bear on the situation.

Next, I did some research on Fish and Wildlife, to see if I could find out any way around this rule. I learned that it began in 1871, in response to a decline in food fish, which is how it got its name. At that time it was called the U.S. Commission on Fish and Fisheries. A similar office, the Division of Biological Survey, was established in 1896. This office focused on the effect of birds in controlling agricultural pests, and on mapping the geographical distribution of plants and animals in the United States. Much later, in 1934, under the direction of Jay Norwood Darling, this became the Bureau of Biological Survey, and began an ongoing legacy of protecting vital natural habitat throughout the country. In 1940 this office was combined with the Bureau of Fisheries, moved to the Department of the Interior, and redubbed the U.S. Fish and Wildlife Service. Today, the agency's mission is "working with others to conserve, protect, and enhance fish, wildlife, plants, and their habitats for the continuing benefit of the American people."

It had done some great things in fulfilling that mission. Even before it was Fish and Wildlife, it was responsible for the Lacey Act, the first federal law protecting game, and for creating the first federal bird reservation under President Theodore Roosevelt. From protecting migratory birds and endangered species to creating extensive wildlife reservations, the agency had certainly done its job, adding its store of good to the world. But everything I read made it clear that its job wasn't bird rescue—at least, not on an individual scale. Fish and Wildlife dealt with systems, with great plans, not one gunshot bird.

Okay, I thought. It is what it is, and you don't ask a horse to be a cow, after all. Still, I was troubled that even though rescue was outside the agency's purview, it could still make rules to prevent rescue. And as far as I could tell, there weren't any official government entities that facilitated rescue. There were other animal rescue organizations, and I got in touch with many of them, but they all had to deal with Fish and Wildlife, too. Every e-mail I sent out to them came back saying my goal was impossible.

I felt much as I had when I was bouncing back and forth between DMV and Social Security. Somehow humans had managed to create a world that stymied reasonable solutions to fairly straightforward problems. Because here, really, was something very simple. The bird was there, and it needed to get here. Certainly it was physically possible to transport it. Planes go back and forth between Afghanistan and the United States all the time. And we had a ready and willing home for the injured bird. But a rule that had little or nothing to do with the current situation blocked us.

The more I learned, the more this began to look like the dilemma of the twenty-first century. With the world grown so large, rules lost their individual application, becoming a standardized pack of words that took no account of particular realities. Standardized tests in education, standardized risk pools in insurance, political polls, and market surveys determine all.

But I was raised by eccentrics and outliers. My Italian grandmother, an immigrant, marched with the suffragettes and bobbed her hair, both risky moves. My mother got a master's degree and worked as a teacher all her life when most women were home in their kitchens. I belonged to those people who didn't even recognize a norm, much less fit in it. Well, I thought, whether it was Pluto or my ancestors asking me to fight a battle for human connection in a depersonalized era, I wanted to do it well.

I'd already gotten political help, so I thought of the other lessons from my experience with Social Security and DMV. Don't take the first "no" as a final answer. And see who you are, be what you see. I am a writer. I would write.

I started by posting a few things on Facebook, just to vent. Then I posted on a few bird rescue and bird-watching sites and community bulletin boards, seeking solutions from anyone who might have a few. Someone might have an idea, or a bit of knowledge I didn't possess. As I was thinking through my next move I got a call from Pete Dubacher, wanting an update.

When I told him the bad news from Fish and Wildlife he wasn't surprised. "They're not easy to deal with. And I wouldn't hold out a lot of hope on getting this done."

To hear this from Pete, the most hopeful of men, was tough, but I wasn't letting go yet. "We have to," I protested. "You know we do."

"Yeah," he agreed, and thought about it some. "Y'know, we ought to talk to my friend Toodie."

Pete's many years of bird rescue had put him in touch with some interesting people, but I didn't know this one. "Toodie?" I asked.

"She's in the city. She does pigeon rescue. She's been a real great supporter for years. And she knows some journalists at the *Post*. Listen, I'll call her, let her know about it. Maybe we can get an article written. That might help."

It just might, I thought. And though I had felt alone and powerless, what Pete said reminded me there were other people in the world who cared about birds. It also reminded me I wasn't the only writer in town. I knew a few others.

I picked up the phone and called one of them, a man named Paul Grondahl, who writes feature articles for the *Albany Times Union.*

CHAPTER 6

Just My Opinion

To: Wekselbaum, Caroline (Schumer)
Sent: Tue, Jun 29, 2010 1:24 am
Subject: RE: Possible Golden Eagle Rescue

All,

    I am not a bird expert, but we now think Eagle Mitch looks like a Steppe Eagle, which would make more sense considering the location. Can someone reexamine the pictures I sent and make a determination of the species?

    . . . I know none of us are involved with the regulations but there is definitely a problem if they are so strict they don't allow the rescue of one bird simply because it wasn't already in the United States. Just my opinion.

Greg Wright

As soon as I put the call in to Paul Grondahl I received the e-mail from Greg suggesting that Mitch wasn't a Golden Eagle but a Steppe Eagle. I let Caroline notify Fish and Wildlife because both of us felt it was best to let her take the diplomatic role, something I'm not particularly good at. Then I waited to see what would happen next. Would there be another regulation blocking Steppe Eagles? Would he have to go to Guantanamo Bay for questioning?

While I braced myself for the next crisis, I contemplated Greg's dry yet pointed response to Fish and Wildlife's denial, and my admiration for him grew. It was so wise and so understated, it gave me an image of him as someone who sees what's right but feels no need to shout about it. That, to me, is a hallmark of maturity—one I don't always have. So often we hear news of war atrocities, about soldiers acting in less than human ways, but Greg's experience had somehow made him grow more human. Of course, Navy SEALs are a special breed, one the country has become more aware of since they took part in the raid that captured Osama bin Laden.

The SEALs, an acronym for "Sea, Air, and Land," were created under the auspices of President John F. Kennedy, who recognized the need for more unconventional fighting forces, but their beginnings trace back to World War II. At that time Scouts and Raiders, Naval Combat Demolition Units, and similar groups of specially trained amphibious fighters saw action in the allied landings in Europe, on the North African coast, at Omaha Beach, Normandy, and in many other crucial fields of battle.

Their training, known as BUD/S (Basic Underwater Demolition/SEALs), is rigorously designed to teach them to meet just about any combat situation. In fact, it's been called torturous, both mentally and physically brutal, like nothing else you would ever choose to go through. Trainees are subjected to what the Navy calls continual calculated harassment, meant to prepare these young men to deal with any crisis, under any amount of physical or mental pressure. On average, only about a third will finish this phase of the training. The rest will ring the brass bell that hangs prominently in the camp, and get out.

To complete the eighteen-to-twenty-four-month training, SEAL hopefuls such as Greg are thrown into the water with their hands and feet tied and told to swim. They brave huge waves in tiny rubber boats and swim five miles at night in waters they're told are shark-infested. And they push themselves through the infamous Hell Week, a continual 132 hours of physical labor that allows only about 4 hours of sleep throughout. During this week they're constantly exhausted, constantly cold and wet, constantly challenged to give up, give up, give up. Ring the bell and go home.

They have to overcome mental as well as physical obstacles. They have to keep thinking, stay smart. Pete Dubacher said to me more than once during the Eagle Mitch saga that he knew Scott and Greg would come up with solutions to the many problems we all faced. He had every confidence they would figure out how to build a crate, how to feed Mitch, how to keep him alive. "They're problem-solvers," he told me. "That's their training. It's who they are."

They're also trained in working as a team rather than alone. Officers and enlisted men go through BUD/S as equals, because one of the primary lessons they must learn is that no one person matters as much as the team, and no one can make it through BUD/S on his own. They learn to check on each other, keep each other awake, cheer each other on through the worst of it. They are utterly reliant on their team to survive, as they will be once they go into combat. And SEALs pride themselves on the fact that they've never left another SEAL behind on a mission.

Greg had been through all this, so his low-key response was really no surprise. But he isn't the kind of person to talk about either his training or the risks he takes. Instead, he just lived it. Did what needed to be done and moved on.

He probably had early examples of that as well, since he grew up in a military family. They moved around a lot, he said, but ultimately ended up in Albuquerque, New Mexico. Out of high school he wasn't sure what to do. He knew he liked the water, and he thought of the coast guard, but while he was in a Naval Academy prep school he learned about the SEALs and decided to go for that. "They're a direct action force, working in small units," he said. "I like direct action."

No surprise there, either.

Greg had already done a few deployments before Eagle Mitch came along, and was familiar with the country, its flat and arid landscape ringed with mountains, reminding him of New Mexico.

"Where Mitch got shot was what you'd call the middle of nowhere," he said, "at the ranges where we train. It's all dirt terrain, with just some small plants dotting the landscape, and some small trenches where water flows sometimes."

That day, on the range, they were using blanks to train Afghan soldiers. Mitch landed down range and a soldier picked up some live ammunition that happened to be there, took a shot at the eagle and hit it. It was, Greg said, a huge deal for live ammo to be used on a range for blanks, and then to shoot an eagle with it—that, he said, was beyond his comprehension. But then, he knew that there was a lack of understanding about the diversity of wildlife in Afghanistan. "They don't think about that kind of thing here. There's so much poverty, it's a very different mindset. And the eagle itself is pretty common, similar to our ravens or crows—no one thought of it as special."

In a country torn by years of war, its people impoverished and struggling to survive, it's no wonder that's the case. However, as Greg told me the story, I thought of Pete Dubacher's Bald Eagle, Eddie, who was shot in Buffalo, New York, because someone wanted to sell his feathers. I mentioned this to Greg and he responded, again low-key, "Yeah. There's no shortage of idiots anywhere, is there?"

There's not. But fortunately there's also a good supply of people like Greg. He got involved because he saw what Scott was doing to care for Eagle Mitch, knew that Scott was paying out of pocket to feed him, so he helped with that. But they were scheduled for deployment back to the United States in just a few months, so they had to do something. And of course, the SEALs never leave a team member behind, even if he happens to be a bird.

Together they began working on that problem, and in the last few months of Eagle Mitch's residence in Afghanistan, Greg handled responsibility for his needs, though he didn't talk about that much either. He gave most of the credit to Scott and to Eileen Jenkins, the veterinarian who cared for Mitch toward the end of his journey.

One thing I learned in dealing with both Scott and Greg is that there's no brag in these guys at all. Low-key, self-effacing, they never spoke about their missions, never saw what they did as anything outside the norm. I knew from others I spoke with that they had both gone through some trouble to keep this bird alive, but they shrugged that off. "You just see what's right, and you do it," Greg said to me.

Simple. Very simple. And not at all easy. At least, not in twenty-first-century America, where complications abound.

Once Greg told us Mitch was probably a Steppe Eagle, Caroline Wekselbaum let Fish and Wildlife know. Ironically, his foreign identity would allow him in, though the rules would keep him out if he were a native breed, a fact I'm still puzzling my way through. Given our attitude toward human immigrants, I somehow would expect the opposite to be true.

But the rules weren't done with us yet. Just as I'd so recently had to prove I was American to get what I needed, now we had to prove Mitch was foreign.

Oh, Lordie, I thought. Another identity issue.

Fortunately Scott and Greg had photos, and responded to requests from Fish and Wildlife for wingspan measurements and whatever else they needed—I'm guessing they would have gotten him a Price Chopper Advantage card and a cable bill if they had to. A great flurry of e-mails and phone calls followed, between Afghanistan and Senator Schumer's office, between that office and Fish and Wildlife, between all of them and me, and between me and Pete Dubacher, who also confirmed from the photos that Mitch was a Steppe Eagle. And then there were more e-mails back and forth dealing with information about when and how he was injured, what facility he was living in now, more measurements and information about his wounds and current status.

After another few days, Fish and Wildlife was willing to confirm that Mitch was who he purported to be, even without a cable bill. But that was just the first step. Next we needed confirmation from veterinarians in Afghanistan, and approval of Berkshire Bird Paradise as his ultimate landing ground, which required lots more paper.

In theory I understood that Fish and Wildlife had to check these things, but Pete had been caring for injured birds for thirty-five years, was known worldwide for his work with eagles, and had numerous licenses Fish and Wildlife had already approved. They knew enough about him to send him a letter when Victoria laid eggs. So couldn't they just reference their own records?

The answer to that was no. They needed all physical specifications of his facility, with photos, copies of his various licenses, specific physical parameters for Mitch's housing, and more. All this information had to be put into the proper forms, which were, to me, practically indecipherable. The gentleman who sent the forms was kind enough to say he knew it looked daunting, but he would walk me through it. And because of Senator Schumer's help, the paperwork had gone to the top very quickly, so we were dealing with the chief of permits. Scary, but in a good way.

Pete suggested that instead of trying to fit the forms we should write a narrative, which suited me just fine. In fact, I live most of my life by narrative, which might explain why I struggle so much with forms. Stories allow for fuller and more accurate description than forms can.

Together we got it all done, but I strongly suspect that Senator Schumer's backing and Caroline's polite coaxing, and her courteous persistence in dealing with the overworked staff of government offices, were of greater value than my narrative skills. What also helped a great deal was Paul Grondahl's article in the *Times Union*, the first of three he would write on Eagle Mitch. As happens these days, his article was reposted on many websites, and it caused a bit of a stir.

Paul, the author of several nonfiction books and a journalist whose writing I greatly admire, had detailed the plight of the eagle and the young men who were taking care of him. He interviewed me for the cranky view of it all, and spent time with Pete Dubacher at Berkshire Bird Paradise. He also interviewed Tom Alvarez, spokesman for Fish and Wildlife's northeast regional office, who outlined a litany of regulations against bringing Mitch to the United States.

A treaty called CITES (signed at the Convention on International Trade and Endangered Species), listed the Steppe Eagle as a bird of "least concern," because it had an estimated worldwide population of ten thousand birds. This treaty also required an export permit from Afghanistan, where Steppe Eagles are prized for hunting. Alvarez thought it unlikely we would get the permit. Even if we did, Mitch would need a U.S. Wildlife Conservation Act permit and an Appendix 2 permit, and more.

Daunting. Yes.

I nurtured my rather extensive capacity for denial and forged ahead, pushing the story as widely as I could, knowing that media support was as valuable as political backing. Pete's friend Toodie got in touch with her friend at the *Post*, and one of their writers interviewed me. After a great flurry of excitement about this, the story appeared as one obscure paragraph, tucked away under a looming celebrity scandal.

I began to revise my theory about what was wrong with the twenty-first-century: it wasn't standardization, but celebrity worship. However, I also got a call from ABC News, to let me know they were tracking the story and wanted me to keep them posted on how it turned out.

"Could be a happy ending, or a train wreck," I told the reporter I spoke with.

"Either way would make a good story," he replied.

Yeah. And I suppose that was one more thing wrong with the twenty-first century.

Meanwhile, Eagle Mitch was not thriving in a war zone, and both Greg and Scott were having difficulties finding the kind of food he needed. Rodents were usually poisoned, and processed food—

even cut-up chicken pieces—didn't provide the kind of nutrients he could get from things like bones and guts. He was losing weight, and Greg and Scott were worried that his time would run out before the regulations did.

As Paul Grondahl's article was posted on the Internet, and media and readers started to respond, I also kept writing.

"I do not," I wrote, "want this bird to die of red tape."

CHAPTER 7

Something Remarkable

From: binnie klein <binniek@comcast.net>
To: chepaitis@aol.com
Sent: Thu, Jul 1, 2010 8:00 pm
Subject: something remarkable

Barbara,

Something remarkable happened after our talk on the radio. I went to my office to see some psychotherapy clients and in the waiting room was a client holding a large cardboard box.

Meekly she held the box out and said "I found a bird on the ground, but. . . . I think it died."

I almost burst into tears. Nothing like this ever occurred before! She came into my office and I told her this was very unusual, since I just spoke with you about birds. She was also astonished by the "coincidence."

I reassured her, using what I learned from you — i.e., "You TRIED; that's the important thing; birds are easily stressed — you didn't do anything wrong."

There was a new and surprising softness in this powerhouse lawyer. I saw a new side of her through this strange event. "I'm able to be more vulnerable about animals than people," she said.

I still can't believe it!

My radio interview about my book, *Feathers of Hope*, had a star-tling follow-up. When Binnie left the interview and returned to her therapy practice she was immediately confronted with a client who brought her a dead bird. What she wrote to me about that interaction confirmed my sense of why Eagle Mitch mattered to Greg and Scott, to all the people I was hearing from on Facebook and other websites.

Birds hold a special place in our hearts, their vulnerability and capacity for flight calling on our deepest sense of compassion and hope. In response to my posts about Eagle Mitch, people offered advice, contacts, moral support. They told their own stories of bird rescues, failed or successful, and wrote about how much it meant to them. How it lifted their hearts when they saw a bird fly away. How sad they were when a bird died. How much solace and wisdom they got just from watching the birds in their yards.

I was touched by the response Mitch's story was getting. It con-firmed my sense that humans are hungry for the kindness inherent in this act, and if we succeeded, we would be feeding many. That helped me deal with the personal injustices I was fielding, and it helped me keep the rescue effort going during a very busy month of July.

I was responding to hundreds of e-mails about Eagle Mitch, from both the growing number of government offices involved and the growing number of people who were interested in Eagle Mitch's cause. At the same time, I was preparing to take on a new teaching job as faculty coordinator for a new low-residency MFA program at Western State College of Colorado. That program would have me living in Gunnison, Colorado, for three weeks, from July to early August,

I was also at the height of promotion for my first nonfiction book, *Feathers of Hope*, which meant I was talking to many people about the human connection with birds. That turned out to be a good thing. The stories I heard from others served to remind me why I was doing this, and how bird rescue encompassed more than just the bird itself.

As I wrote in that book, folktales from around the world, as well as Native wisdom, tell us that birds are our teachers and helpers, sustaining our souls in difficult times. The injured wings of Eagle Mitch had a very broad spread. That also meant I was responsible for more than just my personal need to complete a bird rescue. There were many people who cared about this bird now.

Already he had become a mascot for U.S. troops in Afghanistan, and a wild friend for Greg and Scott, providing them with a reminder of what existed beyond the uncertainties of combat. Scott told me of a day when he watched Mitch jump from his perch into a bowl of water. He dipped his head in and shook it, dipped it in and shook it again. "He had this squirrelly look on his face," Scott said, "like he was thinking, 'I hope no one else saw this, but it sure felt good.' He was really enjoying himself."

Some doctors speak of the importance of "remembered wellness" to people who are experiencing pain. If the body can remember what it feels like to be well, healing occurs more swiftly. And if young men and women stationed in a region of war can witness a bird at his bath in a moment of pure and simple pleasure, they can hold onto what pure and simple pleasures feel like.

Yes. This mattered.

Dr. Eileen Jenkins, an army veterinarian who would take over the care of Mitch much later in the process, told me that as Greg witnessed Mitch's improved health, "his face lit up like a little kid's at Christmas. This big tough guy, a Navy SEAL, and you could just see how much this meant to him. And he wasn't the only one who felt that way."

She was amazed, she said, at how many people in Afghanistan put themselves out for Mitch, until she saw how much they got from doing so. "When you're in a place like Afghanistan surrounded by so much violence, when you have the opportunity to do something good, even in the smallest way, you want to take it. We had people volunteering to clean his cage, people just coming in and asking if they could help in any way."

Part of that she chalked up to a pre-existing interest in doing something good. People who choose to go to Afghanistan already have a sense of purpose, a wish to take part in something larger than themselves. And Eagle Mitch had become something larger. Because of how he was rescued, he had become a symbol of compassion they could get behind.

"We all looked at it and saw that someone like Greg and Scott, a Navy SEAL and Army Ranger trained to be so physical, so aggressive, valued what Mitch had to offer," she said. "Something in them reached out to this helpless animal and wanted only to see him get well. That taught us all something."

In my previous book I speculated that saving a wild creature speaks to our need to nurture what's wild and free in ourselves. In the same way, perhaps seeing what's vulnerable in such a creature touches our own vulnerability, helps us to acknowledge that we are all fragile, and calls us to honor that fragility in ourselves and others.

I also began to hear from others in the armed services about the importance of Eagle Mitch. A friend whose nephew recently went to Iraq heard about him and encouraged me to keep trying to save him. This kind of thing is so important, he said. When you're far from home, surrounded by trouble, and you have the chance to save a creature that needs you, that keeps you human.

Hector Torres, an army sergeant who offered help in finding transport, said the same. "When we save these creatures," he told me, "we're saving our souls." That rang true with me. As a writer who lives more in metaphor than fact, I understood that the flight of a bird is an enduring image of our own souls' capacity to take wing. Mitch, who would never fly again, now needed our wings to save him, and in completing that task, we were caring for all that was good in our own spirits.

That is, if we could complete it.

In spite of our early setback, we all felt hopeful that we could. Our end of the import paperwork for Fish and Wildlife was completed by July thirteenth, and we were pretty assured that they would sign off on it. After that, we figured we only had to get export papers and transportation. While we began looking into that, a few simple and sweet pleasures bolstered the general good mood.

Pete Dubacher was ready to band and release Eagle Victoria's chicks and he asked Scott and Greg if they would like the honor of naming them. Perhaps they'd like to name them after fallen comrades.

Greg said that needed family approval, and it was best not to touch on the painful emotions of family in these cases. But both he and Scott had other suggestions for names. "If you'd name them Snowball and Wally, I'd be honored," Greg said.

Snowball and Wally, he told me, were his two dogs back home in Virginia. He sent me photos of them, two fuzzballs with cheerful faces. He said he couldn't wait to get home and run on the beach with them again. Something else unexpected from a very tough guy.

Scott asked for his eagle chick to be named Britanny, after his wife. Though he didn't mention it until later, she was expecting their first baby.

Those happy events were somewhat overshadowed by concerns for Mitch's health. That Mitch had survived gunshot and living in a war zone was a tribute to his own SEAL-like toughness, but all of us were aware that time mattered. The more paperwork delays we faced, the less chance he had of getting out alive.

Already Scott was trying to deal with Mitch's bumblefoot, a common condition birds get from walking too much on hard, rough surfaces or from perching for too long, which creates small wounds on the bottoms of their feet that can become infected. It's not hard to treat if it's seen early and if the living conditions can be changed enough to prevent recurrence, but changing Mitch's living conditions might take some time and Greg and Scott didn't have access to regular veterinarian care at their base camp. Army veterinarians visited, but then went elsewhere, their responsibilities including care of the many bomb-sniffing dogs in their area, and education in various villages on animal husbandry.

Still, our success with Fish and Wildlife had lifted our spirits, and we thought it shouldn't be much longer before we got Mitch to a better situation. An e-mail from Greg at around this time reflected both our rather naive expectations and our concerns:

> Barbara,
>   That's great on the import papers. Like you said, it sounds like we just need this export permit and then a plane ticket and we're set.

Our medic went by to check up on the vet today and
found out she had to go somewhere else in country for an
unspecified amount of time. I am going to just try to contact
the Ministry of Agriculture myself with one of the interpret-
ers we have here and try to just get it done. If this fails, then
we'll have to rely on the vet's connections because that will
be about the only option we have left. But I'm optimistic and
think it will work out.

Greg, a direct action kind of guy, was still optimistic. So was I.
In fact, I had one more reason to be optimistic, in spite of our concerns. Just after the paperwork for Fish and Wildlife was done, I got on
a train headed for Gunnison, Colorado. I would spend the next three
weeks working with graduate students on my favorite activity: writing. I would also be 1,700 miles from home, two hours behind in time,
with about 80 percent less humidity than I was used to, and about eight
thousand feet higher than normal. I'd be living with people I had never
met before, teaching in a whole new way with a whole new population,
in a culture that's markedly different from my New York state of mind.

And for the first time, I would have a cell phone, something
that would turn out to be crucial in the weeks ahead, as it became
clear that export papers were a lot more difficult to come by than our
optimism made us believe.

CHAPTER 8

Best POC

Barbara,

I have spent some time trying to track down a way to get this bird moved out of Afghanistan. . . . Sadly it is almost impossible to get someone in Afghanistan to do a medical report let alone the necessary CITES work. I have spoken to several colleagues in Europe and the Middle East and no one has a clue on how to do this legally. . . .

Scott
Scott A. Tidmus
AZA Raptor TAG Chair
Disney's Animal Kingdom

Barbara/Caroline,

I've inquired about the best POC for you on this. I will get back to you tomorrow with a contact person, or more information on your request.

Best,
Greta
Greta Lundeberg
Senior Policy Advisor for Afghanistan and Pakistan
Bureau of Legislative Affairs |U.S. Department of State

When I was less than a week into my new teaching job in Colorado, Greg e-mailed me, saying he was having trouble getting in touch with the Afghanistan Ministry of Agriculture, the office we needed for Mitch's export permit. Anything he sent to them had to first get cleared through his higher-ups, and there was no telling how long that would take, or if his e-mail would produce any results.

News from Caroline was no more encouraging. Her work was primarily domestic, and this was an international question. For my part, I didn't have a clue how to proceed. I also didn't have much time at my disposal to figure it out. My very intense summer session included morning trainings, daytime classes, and evening readings, along with the usual socialization that's so important in this kind of program. My time was limited, and my mental resources fully engaged.

But I was uncomfortable with the notion of just waiting for Greg's veterinarian to return. I'm not, in general, very good at waiting, though writers do an awful lot of it. So late at night I opened my laptop and searched for ways to contact the U.S. embassy in Afghanistan. That produced an e-mail address and a phone number, and I used both, sending an e-mail and leaving a voice message. No one ever responded, and to this day I wonder what they thought about getting a message from a woman who asked about saving an eagle.

I also called Pete Dubacher to let him know what was going on. "That's a tough one," he said. "But y'know, you got this far, so I'm guessing you'll come up with something."

Something. But what?

I started posting on Facebook, tweeting on Twitter, and getting in touch with some of the contacts that came my way. I sent an e-mail to a contact I got from Sue, Pete's e-mail liaison. This man worked for Disney, procuring their live animals and caring for them. I sent e-mails to Greenpeace, and to a few other international animal rescue organizations, to see what they knew about exporting birds.

The replies were discouraging. Most said it was impossible. The rest said it was near enough to impossible as to make no difference. Some people suggested we leave Mitch at the Kabul Zoo at least temporarily. But Greg had looked into that earlier, and now he sent us some articles about that facility.

An article from the *Christian Science Monitor* (http://www.csmonitor.com/2005/0811/p07s01-wosc.html) said the zoo had once been the frontline in Afghanistan's factional fighting, and now had become "a virtual torture chamber for the animals which survived the strife." Zookeepers said they were weary of telling visitors to "stop torturing the animals." Several had died after being beaten or fed narcotics by visitors. Taliban soldiers were particularly fond of baiting the animals, leaping on the cages, and cutting tree branches to poke and hit them. The article offered the image of the lone remaining black bear, "munching forlornly on an empty pack of cigarettes."

A similar article in the *Los Angeles Times* (http://articles.latimes.com/2009/dec/27/world/la-fg-afghan-zoo27-2009dec27) said that the zoo was "wounded," an extension of a country wounded by decades of war. The zoo director at the time told them, "The big problem with our country is that no one knows what to do with the animals. The war has damaged their minds." Pointing out a moat of filthy water filled with trash that surrounded the macaques, he said, "They fight with the animals. They don't just come to see them."

A sign put up to discourage bad behavior read, "Dear Citizens: The animals are creatures of God. While watching them, please avoid annoying or bothering them."

It didn't sound like a good prospect. Not at all. And it was clear to me that the guys wanted Mitch at Pete's sanctuary, where even badly injured eagles go on to live for another thirty years.

While I was fretting about the situation in a phone conversation with my son he said, "You should try Hillary."

"Friend of yours?" I asked.

"Hillary Clinton," he said. "You know. Secretary of State? I'm guessing she'd know who to talk to."

My husband said the same thing. Hillary. Or at least the U.S. Department of State. This was their purview.

Okay. The State Department.

I tried to imagine myself explaining this situation to people who deal with issues of world power on a daily basis. I tried to imagine getting anyone to listen to me. It didn't seem feasible. Just as the Steppe Eagle is a bird of least concern in the world of Fish and Wildlife, I am a person of least concern in politics.

Still, like every other government entity, the State Department has a website, and Hillary had a slot for sending e-mail to her. Somewhere around one a.m., as I was still awake and writing about an eagle, I sent her an e-mail, with little hope that she would answer it. But while I was on the website I also started looking up other State Department offices, trying to figure out which one would field questions about export papers for a war-wounded eagle. Economics and Energy? Definitely not. Public Diplomacy? Didn't look good. Travel warnings—it was way too late for any warning. Democracy and Global Affairs looked promising, maybe under the subheading "Refugees." But after skimming through it, I didn't find anything about refugee eagles.

By two a.m. I was too frustrated to be tired. I clicked on the "Contact us" link and got the main number of the State Department, deciding I would call in the morning and hope to get through to someone.

Keeping the time difference in mind, I knew I would have to make my calls somewhere between meetings and class, so at around noon I scurried back to my dorm room with my cell phone and called the State Department.

The automated system frightened me. When my husband was dealing with unemployment I often heard him in his office cursing and muttering. He was told to call a certain number, and when he did, he was directed to punch in a series of numbers, which put him back at the beginning of the menu, where he was told to punch in a series of numbers, which . . .

You get the idea. So when I called the State Department I didn't know what kind of phone hell waited for me. As it turned out, their automated menu was pretty easy, and though my issue didn't fit any of their specific offices (there's no State Department office for international bird rescue), it allowed me to simply dial zero and speak with a human.

Blessed relief. A human voice. Neutral, female, not cheery or friendly, but human. I went into what would become my standard speech. "Hi. I'm Barbara Chepaitis. I'm an author and I'm trying to help some U.S. troops stationed in Afghanistan with an eagle they rescued after it was shot. They're trying to get it back to the U.S., and I need to help them figure out how to get the right export papers from the Ministry of Agriculture in Afghanistan. Can you direct me to the right office?"

I said my speech as quickly as possible and then I waited. There was a long pause.

"A—bird?" the voice asked.

"An eagle," I amended.

"Oh. Well—I'm not—hmm. And what did you say your name is?"

"Barbara. Barbara Chepaitis. I'll spell it for you." Often at this point in a conversation I was tempted to spell it S-M-I-T-H just so see if the person on the other end noticed. This time I resisted the urge.

"I don't really have any idea who you could talk to about that here," the woman said, sounding distracted. This wasn't high on the radar screen for important calls. Just a crazy bird lady. "Have you tried Department of Defense?"

"I don't think that would help," I said. "I need someone who knows about export papers for wildlife, and how to get them. These two young men—one of them's a Navy SEAL—they've been taking care of this poor bird for months. They've done so much for him, and they just want to get him to a safe place."

"I'm still not sure . . ."

"If you need to, you can speak with Caroline Wekselbaum in Senator Schumer's office. He's been helping us."

At this, there was no pause. "I'm going to put you through to Brad Parker," she said. "He may be able to help."

Okay, then. Now I knew how to open doors at the State Department. And I didn't forget. From then on, any call I made regarding

Eagle Mitch started this way: "Hi. I'm Barbara Chepaitis. I'm working with Senator Schumer's office to help our U.S. troops rescue an eagle. . . ." That sentence was the great expediter, lending credibility to a crazy bird lady with a problem that didn't fit the forms.

Brad wasn't in, but I left a message on his voicemail and went on to send out a few more e-mails and put a few more posts on community bulletin boards about animal rescue. Sooner or later someone would get back to me. I hoped.

And that afternoon I did something I had never done before. I brought my cell phone to class and left it on. I've always forbidden cell phones in the classroom, so I felt like the ultimate hypocrite, but if by chance Hillary did call, I wanted to be available. Then I debated how to explain that.

My students, all impressively skilled writers, were still getting comfortable with graduate work, and with the exposure that comes when put your writing in front of peers and professionals. And they were all from a western culture, one that prefers not to be too loud, too much trouble, or too exposed. Already they'd given me quite the eye when we talked about writing from the heart of your own emotions.

"I don't express myself personally in my work," one of them told me. "I just don't do that."

"That's, um, interesting," I said, confused. As a writer, I believed in living your work, and working your life. The two were inextricably intertwined for me, and there wasn't much about my own life I wasn't willing to use, if it served the needs of a book. And here I was, about to become a living example of how your writing and your life can get all tangled up in situations way beyond your ken. I hoped it didn't terrify them.

"Sorry about the cell phone," I told them. "I'm waiting for a call about this eagle. I'm helping some troops in Afghanistan get it here because one of my books is about the sanctuary they want to send it to." That seemed brief, professional, not at all personal. Nothing about being up until after two a.m. trying to get in touch with the State Department. Nothing about how terrified of failing I was, or

about how my next move, if this didn't work, was to give Paul Grondahl a call for another article.

"You're what?" one of them asked, and I explained further. This
time I think I got an edge in my voice, some of my frustration with
the process coming out in my tone. One of the women had a son in
service and was sympathetic, so I talked at greater length about how
writing a book can lead you places you never thought you'd go, and
what it means to go there, or to choose not to.

"It *is* personal, what we do," I said, thinking of our previous
discussion. "In fact, it's really important to be able to put it out there,
make a fool of yourself, be loud." They were looking nervous, but I
carried on. "So let's howl," I said.

They cast glances at each other, frowned at me. "Howl?"

"Yeah. I need a good howl today. You ever hear the coyotes
howling around here? Think of something that's bugging you and
howl."

Their voices, soft at first, tried out a few yips. "Come on," I said,
and quoted Arlo Guthrie. "You wanna change the world and shit,
you gotta be louder than that. Think of something that really bugs
you. Or, if you prefer, something that makes you really happy. On the
count of three."

They put their heads back, opened their mouths, and howled,
doing me proud. Then we all laughed about it, and went back to more
traditional classroom activities. We weren't far along when my cell
phone rang. It was Brad Parker, from the State Department.

My students took a break. I took the call. Brad was very helpful,
listening to my story, telling me he would look into it and get back
to me. The next day Caroline and I both got e-mails from Greta Lundeberg, the State Department's senior policy advisor for Afghanistan
and Pakistan, who said she was finding the best point of contact to
resolve this. She contacted Dave Lawson, Wildlife Conservation Society representative in Afghanistan.

You may know this group. They regularly send promotional
mail, asking for donations for membership. Sometimes they include
address labels. Probably you use the labels and move on, not learning

much about who they actually are or what they do. I used to do that myself. I don't do that anymore.

WCS was founded in 1895 to "save wildlife and wild places across the globe." They had helped the American bison recover on the western plains and continued to protect wild things, including gorillas in the Congo, tigers in India, and wolverines here at home, along with creatures of the sea. During their 115 years of existence they had also created a global conservation network, managing projects in more than sixty countries. Their parks include the Bronx Zoo, the New York Aquarium, the Central Park Zoo, Prospect Park Zoo, and the Queens Zoo. They're busy people.

Currently their mission includes a commitment to protecting 25 percent of world biodiversity, addressing issues of climate change, natural resource exploitation, the connection between wildlife health and human health, and the sustainable development of human livelihoods. All this, while they manage more than two hundred million acres of protected lands around the world. They do this because they believe, as I do, that humans living in harmony with wildlife is essential to our integrity.

And they had a desk in Afghanistan, where they helped create that country's first national park, Band-e-Amir. This site, a tourist destination before the Soviet-Afghan war of the 1970s, has six azure blue lakes surrounded by red cliffs and white dams of travertine, a natural mineral deposit of the area. Decades of war, human suffering, and environmental degradation changed all that, but the WCS is still fighting the good fight, hoping to keep it all alive.

I guessed that Dave Lawson had his hands full, but when I sent him an e-mail about Eagle Mitch's situation he responded quickly and confidently, asking for details about where Mitch was found and the circumstances of his injury. He would have to explain all that to the Ministry of Agriculture before making a recommendation to let Mitch go to the United States. With that, he said, getting export papers was relatively simple, though it could take time. He added that in case of delays I should tell Greg and Scott not to worry. They could always send Mitch to his care. He had experience as a falconer, and knew how to tend to such birds.

I wrote the necessary e-mails to Dave, to Greg and Scott, and to Caroline, and then I held my breath, wondering how long this would take, or if Dave could actually deliver. Feeling as if we were in good hands, kind and generous hands, I lived in a state of readiness for the next crisis, the next message of "it can't be done."

As I waited, another small triumph boosted my morale. My students took active part in the open mike at the Writing in the Rockies conference, reading very personal and passionate works. They also howled with vigor to cheer each other on. After our class howling session, they had named themselves the Wolf Pack.

The wings of Eagle Mitch, a Steppe Eagle more than six thousand miles away, had already brushed against their souls, and it was good. He would do the same for others, including myself, encouraging me to stretch my own wings in many ways, not the least of which was in learning more about Afghanistan, and about Steppe Eagles.

CHAPTER 9

The Eagle Plunged

One league he dropped him down
Then the eagle plunged and caught him in his wings.
A second league he dropped him down
Then the eagle plunged and caught him in his wings,
A third league he dropped him down
Then the eagle plunged and caught him in his wings,
Within three cubits of earth
The eagle plunged, and caught him in his wings,

The Myth of Etana

I had learned a thing or two about bald eagles when I wrote *Feathers of Hope*, but I knew nothing about Steppe Eagles, also known as *Aquila nipalensis*. Online research told me some basic facts—that the Steppe is a common bird, breeding in Romania and eastward through the southern Russian and central Asian steppes to Mongolia. The European and central Asian birds winter in Africa, and the eastern birds in India. They favor open, dry habitats, such as desert, semi-desert, steppes, or savannah.

Though the Steppe Eagle was once classified as a subspecies of the Tawny Eagle, morphology, behavior, and DNA studies showed it to be its own particular species, larger and darker than the Tawny

Eagle, with a pale throat lacking in that species. It is also migratory, while the Tawny Eagle is not. It eats carrion and whatever small prey it can catch.

That's how it exists in nature. Its relationship to humans is as complex as that of any other eagle. Steppe Eagles, used in falconry, are known to be intelligent, inquisitive, and curious birds. One appears on the coat of arms of Saladin, whose forces defeated the Crusaders and led the way to his recapture of Palestine after eighty-eight years of Crusader rule in the twelfth century. Saladin's chivalrous behavior was noted by Christian chroniclers, and he won the respect of many Crusaders, including Richard the Lionheart. His eagle now appears on the Egyptian flag.

And the country of Kazakhstan calls its joint Kazakh-NATO annual military exercise "Steppe Eagle." This exercise trains combined forces for combat readiness, its main goal for the Kazakh army to become NATO qualified in both peacekeeping and humanitarian missions.

After I learned all that, I went in search of what folktales and myths I might find about Steppe Eagles. As humans, we tend to define our world through stories, and stories are patterned things, clearly shaped structures that contain the important lessons of a culture. When I was talking to editors about the Eagle Mitch story, many of them scrunched up their editorial noses and said, "It's a good story, but it's not *warm*. You know, like dog stories." Couldn't I make it more doggie-like, they wanted to know.

No, I said. I can't. Not unless I lie.

It's an eagle story, not a dog story. It has a whole different pattern, a whole different purpose. Dog stories are about loyalty and caring for what's loyal to us, because dogs are, by their nature, loyal. Eagles, on the other hand, are wild, majestic, noble, and fierce in their willingness to hang on when necessary. I talked about the mating rituals of Bald Eagles, when the male and female soar high in the air, grabbing each other's talons and spinning to earth as they hang on, only letting go at the last possible moment. I pointed out that the Bald Eagle existed as an important emissary for indigenous people long before the first European arrived on the continent. The Haudono-saunee of the Northeast saw them as messengers of the Creator, far-seeing, clear-sighted. They were, and still are, guardians of the Great Peace, sitting perched at the top of the Tree of Peace in constant vigil.

Raptors, who hold us hostage with the intensity of their gaze, remind us of the potential power and nobility in our own souls, as we try to rise above whatever keeps us rooted in pettiness. Their stories serve to teach us the difference between using our power well, and using it badly.

Most publishers scratched their heads at my enthusiastic and geeky polemic. Most said something about market values in a dif-ficult economy and walked away. Fortunately, James Peltz at SUNY Press thought it was a really cool story that should be told, which was another reminder to me that there are still good people in a wicked world. And then I found an ancient myth that said it all: the Myth of Etana, a Sumerian story dating back to about 2300 BCE.

The story starts with local deities who are searching for a good king to rule the land of Kish after the great flood. The goddess Ishtar believes a man named Etana is the right guy for the job, and the oth-ers agree. He becomes king, and promptly builds a shrine to Ishtar and the sun god Shamash, near a poplar tree. As it happens, an eagle has a nest high in the branches of this tree. A serpent has made a home in its roots.

Perhaps inspired by their sacred site, the eagle and serpent de-cide to cooperate with each other, and swear an oath of loyalty that the eagle will guard the serpent's children when he searches for food, and the serpent will do the same for the eagle. All is well until the eagle's children no longer need protection. Then the eagle reneges on his side of the bargain. He eats the serpent's children, though his own children cry out warnings against such a betrayal.

When the serpent returns to find his children gone he appeals to Shamash to punish the eagle, and Shamash agrees. What the eagle did was just plain wrong. Shamash works with the serpent to prepare a trap, and lures the eagle with the carcass of a wild ox, instructing the serpent to wait inside it. When the eagle comes to eat, the serpent seizes him, clips his wings, and throws him into a pit Shamash has prepared for him.

Helpless and imprisoned in the earth, the eagle now cries to Shamash for forgiveness, and apparently Shamash has already figured out a way to teach the eagle a lesson and solve another problem at the same time.

While the eagle has been injured and imprisoned, King Etana has also been petitioning Shamash because he has no son, no heir for his throne. Shamash, in a response that seems at first to be a mythological non sequitur, sends Etana to the eagle, and the two stay in the pit together, perhaps commiserating on their bad fortune and bad choices.

Etana and the eagle become friends, the eagle interpreting Etana's dreams for him. Etana, for his part, develops sympathy for the eagle, feels badly for his wounds, and heals him as best he can. While he does, he dreams repeatedly that he ascends to heaven, where the goddess Ishtar gives him the Plant of Birth, so his wife can have a son. The eagle interprets this as a message from the gods, and he tells Etana he will bring him to the heavens, where he can speak with Ishtar.

Etana clings to the eagle's underbelly, and the eagle, healed by his human friend, flies up and up toward heaven. Etana hangs on, but when he looks down he's terrified, and cries out, "I cannot see the land or the sea! Bring me back!" In his terror, he lets go of the eagle and plunges to earth. The eagle dives down and rescues him before he hits the ground.

Since everything in a story has to happen at least three times— mostly, I think, because it takes humans that long to learn a lesson— three times Etana and the eagle ascend, three times Etana lets go, and three times the eagle rescues him.

Then, on the fourth try, Etana overcomes his fear and the man and the eagle make it to the realm of Ishtar.

The ancient text breaks off at this point, but we can safely assume the goddess was generous, because Etana is recorded as having a son, Balikh, and his dynasty continued for many generations to follow.

There were parts of this story that made my skin prickle with the kind of excitement only a true story geek gets from a text that's numinous with archetypal imagery. The first striking element is the fact that the serpent is the good guy, and the eagle is the betrayer. That goes against most other stories our culture gives us, so it takes some pondering.

I've been taught that in folktales and myth, each character is a piece of one whole psyche that's attempting to integrate itself, and the events of the story make that integration happen. The story of Etana asks us to remember that while our eagle—our powerful, cerebral selves—holds the high ground, our more earthbound selves, like the serpent, can't be betrayed without consequence. Though the eagle flies high, he must ground his power in relation to others, or his earthier self will surely clip his wings and ground him in less pleasant ways.

The eagle learns the lesson of relatedness through responding to the needs of a fearful, earthbound human—one who may be a king but is also just a guy who needs to chat with the goddess, balancing out the male and female energy of his own soul. And he does so by digging into the earth with the wounded eagle.

Etana, of course, won't get the gifts of the goddess unless he compassionately heals the broken wings of another. As in many stories, it's clear that in healing others, we always heal the corresponding broken part of ourselves.

And Etana's fear at rising toward heaven is something most humans have felt in one way or another. When we leave our known emotional or geographical map to enter new territory there's always a time between the start of the journey and the destination when what we've left is gone, but we can't yet see the new land. We are nowhere, and we're just plain scared. At that point, if we let go, it's the task of our newly healed raptor self to dive to our rescue and make sure the journey is completed.

Reading it, I think of the powerful young men who saved Eagle Mitch, who consented to take on his broken wings and stay with him in his earthbound pit. I think of how Mitch was wounded, and I think of the compassion of Pete Dubacher at Berkshire Bird Paradise, of how he's been called the Mother Teresa of birds.

I think of my own journey, the broken part of my wings, and how they were being healed in my own attempts to save this eagle. I wonder if Greg and Scott are aware of broken places in themselves that they're healing as they show compassion to a wounded bird. Offhand I'm guessing not, but the beauty of this situation is that they don't have to. Intellectualizing, analyzing, tends to stay in the head. We heal most thoroughly by doing the work itself.

And I think of larger issues: our need as a nation to remember that we must stay in grounded relationship with others if we're to use our power well, our need to remember how utterly dependent we are on the health and well-being of the land that nurtures us. We may, as a culture, fear the serpent, but the earthly realm of that creature is what made us great. Our resources, our abundant land and all its creatures, make everything else possible, and if we renege on our pact with the land, we'll suffer the consequences.

We are a people who dream big and look far, seeking the stars, but we can't forget that all of us are earthbound creatures. Even those on top, those with the most money and power, had better not forget their dependence on the ones who live at the roots of the tree.

The Myth of Etana helped me to ground myself within the clarity of a narrative, teaching me more of what I needed to do with Eagle Mitch: Hang on. Be prepared to nosedive now and then. Respond with both compassion and strength.

I was fortunate to meet other people who understood all this intuitively, and acted accordingly.

When I sent the contact information for Dave Lawson of WCS to Scott and Greg, Scott responded quickly, saying he'd be glad to help in any way Dave needed. "We have limited resources at my location," he wrote, "but I am sure that whatever it is we need for the export process we can find a way to make it happen."

And to my amazement, word came back from Dave within two days. For once, it was good news. He'd just returned from the Ministry of Agriculture, and had already drafted the required CITES permit and sent it to the appropriate officers with information on how they should complete it. Because the United States had imposed more stringent conditions for CITES permits than other countries, Mitch needed to be inspected by an authorized and competent authority at point of export. Dave told the Ministry he would be available to go to the airport and assist in that inspection.

Personal service, for sure. But Dave also said his job was merely expediting, and gave all kudos to Hasim Barikzai, head of the Natural Resource Management division, and Ghayor Ahmadyar, head of protected areas. The prompt response of these men made all the difference. Here in the Unites States, he said, we don't know enough about how dedicated such men are, working in very difficult circumstances to get the job done. Certainly they'd done so for us, with great speed and efficiency.

In fact, I was astonished. After we'd been told by so many people that export was impossible, they went ahead and did it, as easy as walking on water. And they took it as just a normal part of their day. Just stealing their pay.

As often as I was finding trouble on this journey, I was also finding real heroes. That was incredibly reassuring. While I participated in a weekend conference at the college I was cheering for those heroes and what they'd done for a war-wounded bird. I sincerely hoped the goddess would reward them accordingly.

And I was celebrating. We were good to go, and I could finally start planning the actual flight home. Our ascent would be swift and sure now, with no more accidental plunges toward earth.

Right?

Right?

Scott and Mitch become friends

Mitch in dress uniform

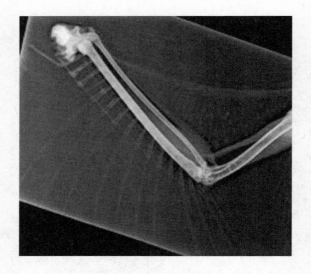

Mitch on the inside

Mitch's digs in Afghanistan

Mitch on his feet again

Proud Mitch

Mitch, needing help

A war victim of a different kind

The Eagle, landing

Pilots N Paws heroes

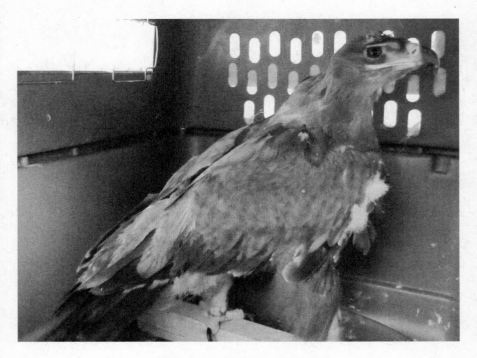

THIS KENNEL CONTAINS A LIVE EAGLE. DO NOT BANG ON THE KENNEL, AVOID TALKING LOUDLY NEAR IT, AND IF MOVING IT, USE EXTREME CARE.

TWO PERSON CARRY ONLY.

Mitch's kennel label

Mitch goes to a new home

Mitch's travel crate, after a long journey

Pete Dubacher welcomes Mitch

Mitch's new home, Berkshire Bird Paradise

Mitch flaps his wings

Mitch's new friend Eddie

Mitch and Eddie

Friends

CHAPTER 10

I Cannot Hold Out Any Hope

USDA Animal and Plant Health Inspection Services

Import Procedures for a Pet Bird Entering (Non-U.S. Origin) the United States

ADVISORY: Until further notice, there is a temporary ban on the importation of all live avian species from Afghanistan, Albania, Azerbaijan, Bangladesh . . .

I celebrated Mitch's export permit on a Sunday night, at the Writing in the Rockies Conference. My fellow faculty members congratulated me. My newly christened Wolf Pack applauded me—and howled. I felt a great weight falling from my shoulders. That night, I fell asleep with a relaxed consideration of transportation options and thoughts of getting Mitch's Berkshire Bird Paradise housing prepared.

On Monday morning, I woke to an e-mail from Caroline, saying she was worried because it looked like the USDA might be a problem.

I called her. She was a little uncertain about it all, still trying to get in touch with someone at USDA to find out how big a problem we had on our hands, but she said it didn't look good. They probably wouldn't allow Mitch to enter the United States.

I have a large capacity for denial, and I worked it hard. Everything in me pushed this thought away, as fast as possible. Besides, I didn't understand what the USDA had to say about it. All I knew about them was that they inspected my food, and that one of their officials had recently been in the news for saying something that was interpreted as racially prejudiced.

"Why are they involved?" I asked Caroline. "They're Department of Agriculture. Nobody's going to eat Mitch."

"It's the avian flu," she told me. "USDA has a ban against bird import from that area because it's endemic there."

"It's not an import, it's a rescue," I pointed out once more.

"That's a distinction they don't make," Caroline said, remaining calm.

My stomach was beginning to get in a twist. "What kind of ban?" I asked.

"Total," she said.

I couldn't, wouldn't believe that. My stomach kept twisting, but I set my jaw and moved on. "What should I do?" I asked.

"I'll keep trying to get in touch with someone at USDA. Their phone system's a little complicated. You can try too, if you want."

I didn't want. What I wanted was for the celebration to continue, but that didn't seem to be in my stars, where Pluto was apparently still challenging me, asking me to nosedive back to earth a few more times. "I'll make some calls," I said.

Caroline sent me the link to the USDA website, where I could see what they had to say, and find a phone number to dial. When I looked at it, even my healthy denial collapsed. USDA did indeed have a total ban of all import of birds from Afghanistan. There it was, in black and white. This was more than a nosedive. I felt like I'd been thrown into the ocean, with my hands and legs tied. And I wasn't swimming. I was sinking. Slowly.

But part of me continued to protest. This wasn't an import. It was a rescue. Mitch wasn't going into the general public. He was going to a bird sanctuary. And they could test him, make sure he was clean. Every rule had to have some kind of exception. All I had to do was find it.

My previous success with the State Department and the absolute lack of response I got to various e-mails made me decide to try for a phone call. It's best, I had learned, to speak with an actual human whenever possible. But first, of course, I had to teach my class.

I went to it glowering, and my Wolf Pack picked up on my mood. That not-expressing-personal-emotions thing was out the window, so I allowed myself a few minutes of vitriolic venting about the situation, then went on with class. I hoped I was setting an example of what it really means to be a writer, but I had my doubts.

After class I had a conversation with my husband, whose job search hadn't yet produced anything. We were in a stagnant economy, and he worked in social welfare programs, one of the hardest-hit areas. The news was talking about AIG people going to spas, and my husband and I, like many other American citizens, were sweating it out. We would probably be able to make our mortgage payments, barring other catastrophes, so we were among the lucky ones. But everything in the world seemed wrong. Simply wrong.

I went from that conversation to the evening faculty readings, evening conversations with students. When I got back to my room, I started my late-night search for USDA phone numbers, in no mood for it. I didn't even know which of the many offices I needed to contact, so I just kept writing down phone numbers, figuring I'd call them all, hoping one of them gave a damn about an eagle that two young men in service wanted to save.

I debated e-mailing Greg and Scott to let them know we were in trouble, but I couldn't face it. The words I would have to say were too painful, too much about failure. I deferred the task.

By two a.m. I headed for bed, but I slept restlessly, plagued by voices telling me I was a fool, on a fool's errand, destined for failure. The ghost of every bird that ever died on my watch came back to visit me. In the brief moments when I dipped into REM sleep, I dreamt of large men in blue suits, who were all laughing at me.

In the morning, before class, I started making phone calls. My first ones were absolutely unproductive. One office I called put me on hold and went away. Another one said, "An eagle. An eagle? I don't know anything about that," and hung up.

A few other numbers, including the Washington, DC, office for the Animal and Plant Health Inspection Service, led me to voicemail, and I left messages. In each one, I made sure to say that I was working with Senator Schumer, and to mention repeatedly that we were doing this for young men in Afghanistan, our troops, who wanted Eagle Mitch saved, and also that ABC News was tracking the story. I think if I'd had a deal with the devil on it I would have mentioned that as well.

In class my Wolf Pack asked for the update on the situation, and I muttered something about imminent disaster and fatigue. They showed concern, sympathy, a shared sense of frustration, which I appreciated. Though I continued to keep my phone available, I received no calls during class.

Then, after dinner, as I was walking back to my dorm room, my phone rang.

I opened it, and the woman's voice on the other end asked if this was Barbara Che—Che—

"Chepaitis," I said. "Yes, this is Barbara."

"This is Dr. Bettina Cooper, from the USDA. I had a message from you, about an eagle in Afghanistan?"

I took a breath and dove in, once again giving my small speech about Eagle Mitch. When I was done, Dr. Cooper spoke politely, with reservation, sounding reluctant to give me bad news.

"The avian flu makes this impossible," she said as gently as she could. Then, brightening, she added, "But there is another way. If you can get the eagle to a country that doesn't have the ban—maybe Germany—if he established residence for ninety days, we may be able to bring him to the Unites States from there."

She sounded like such a nice woman, and I knew she was trying to help. In spite of that, what I wanted to do was scream and spit. Germany? The country that produced Hitler will take this eagle and we won't? And then what—after ninety days he can vote? Buy a house? Get a green card? A Price Chopper Advantage card? By then he'd be dead. And so would I.

I didn't say any of that. I remained professional and explained that Mitch's physical condition was precarious, and he wouldn't survive that kind of stress. We really needed to get him to qualified care in the United States as soon as possible. "These young men did a very compassionate thing, under the most enormous pressure. And they're our troops. Surely we can do this for them," I cajoled. "Couldn't we have Mitch tested for avian flu? There must be tests."

She said we could, but that wouldn't help, something which left me truly baffled.

Again, I wanted to scream, to howl, to lay down on the ground and kick my heels. But I couldn't, because another part of me was in total collapse, the walls of my denial broken at last. I had hoped for something more from this phone call. I had hoped for a solution. And frankly, I hoped to be able to stop fighting for a bird, and move on with other parts of my life.

I was tired. Very tired. I'd been on emotional overload for a long time—since well before my mother's death, in fact—and that overload had only gotten worse when my husband lost his job. The wrongness of the world was infecting my soul, giving me a kind of spiritual bumblefoot. And I was working overtime physically as well, as my body struggled with lack of sleep and the lack of oxygen that came with Colorado's high altitude.

In that brief moment of total fatigue, old voices in my head scolded me. This is a bird, they said. Just a bird. You're fighting for nothing important. Just let it go. You're not the kind of person who can win this battle anyway. You're just a little white woman from a small town, a person of least importance. What you want is no more worthwhile than a wounded bird.

Ring the bell, those voices said. Thank Dr. Cooper, close your cell phone and walk away. Then you can get out of Hell Week and get some sleep. There's no shame in being defeated by forces so much bigger than you. Everyone will understand.

In that moment, all those voices had their say, and then the other part of my mental committee chimed in. It reminded me that Greg got through his SEAL training and was serving in a war zone. That Scott survived Army Ranger training and Iraq, and was doing what he needed to do to take care of his family. That Mitch survived a betrayal of human trust, and was in need of healing and a home. What they did was really tough. All I had to do was deal with the USDA. My fatigue and frustration, my most ancient personal neuroses, weren't at all important in comparison.

When I replied to Dr. Cooper, for the first time in months I was totally calm, totally confident.

"Dr. Cooper," I said, "I want the USDA to rethink its position. These young men did the right thing, and as American citizens, as humans, we need to support that. I have every confidence we can get this done, and I want you to help me do so."

There was a pause on the other end. The kind voice of this woman I didn't know spoke sadly. "I can't hold out any hope," she said. "I don't think it's possible."

Hope, I thought, is the thing with feathers. So Emily Dickinson said. And I had feathers, which meant I still had hope.

"I think it is," I said, with an assurance I didn't know the source of. "I'll be looking into ways to do so, and I'd like it if you did the same."

That was the end of our conversation, in personal terms one of the most important I'd ever had. In it, I had met a source of power and challenged it, not in anger or denial or heat. Instead, I stated a simple truth, something I knew to be right, and made a commitment to continue working toward that end. There was more strength in that than in any other statement I had made so far, because it acknowledged the reality of a difficult and often wicked world, but also named my most deeply held sense that something better was possible, beyond all rational evidence to the contrary.

Later on, much later, when I actually had time to think, I asked myself where those alternate voices in my head came from. What in my life had taught me to ask the USDA to rethink its position? For an eagle? A bird of least concern?

I realized there wasn't just one thing, but an accumulation of lessons from many sources. My mother's insistence on continued, lifelong learning was in there, as was my father's teaching on the importance of responsibility to the environment and its creatures. Pete Dubacher's compassion, and my husband's inviolable integrity, were part of the mix. And there were people at the outer edges of my life, people whose lives and work gave me words to articulate what I believed in my most nonverbal soul.

There was Wendell Berry, whose poem "Manifesto: The Mad Farmer Liberation Front," advises us, "Be joyful, though you have considered all the facts." There were the folk singers Magpie, who wrote a song called "Hawk and Eagle," which says, "To make this mountain journey is no easy climb." Their friends, folk singers Kim and Reggie Harris, who wrote a song called "All My Relations." The chorus says, "A voice from on high says give it one more try. All my relations, speak to my soul."

Yes. All my relations. Including an injured eagle from Afghanistan.

Though it was a small thing, just one bird, and the world wouldn't change as a result, I knew this was important. I wouldn't back down from that. As Pete Dubacher said about addling Eagle Victoria's eggs, they'd have to hang me first.

Not that I was any less tired, mind you. I just knew that being tired didn't matter. As the SEALs say during Hell Week, if you don't mind, it doesn't matter.

I no longer minded.

That evening I e-mailed Paul Grondahl to let him know the USDA was blocking Eagle Mitch's progress. I e-mailed Caroline, and a few other people involved in the situation, to see if they had any advice at all. I posted on Facebook and Twitter, and all the community bulletin boards I'd been keeping up with lately. Then I went to the website for the White House and started looking up phone numbers.

I sent an e-mail to President Obama, to Jon Stewart at *The Daily Show* and Stephen Colbert at *The Colbert Report* and to David Letterman, figuring I would never get an answer but knowing it had to be done. Then I started looking up other White House offices that might have an interest in foreign eagles, in our troops, in anything remotely related.

As I flipped through various offices and their responsibilities I came across something called the Office of Public Engagement, an office created by President Obama.

The White House says that OPE is "the open front door to the White House," "the embodiment of the President's goal of making government inclusive, transparent, accountable and responsible." The mission of this office is to "coordinate opportunities for direct dialogue between the Obama Administration and the American public . . . ensuring that everyone can participate and inform the work of the President."

They wanted, they said, to make sure that "our nation's proud and diverse communities [would have] their voices heard," and that "their concerns [would] be translated into action by the appropriate bodies of the Federal Government."

That sounded right to me. They had a place where you could send an e-mail, but I wanted to speak with someone, because I'd found that a conversation with a human was worth more than a thousand e-mails. However, finding a phone number wasn't easy. I clicked link after link, seeking the right way to get in touch, and finally decided to use the main White House phone number and punch my way through automated menus until I got where I wanted.

All that would have to wait until morning, however. I scribbled down phone numbers and fax numbers and bookmarked URLs, then made my way to restless sleep.

The next morning I was able to connect to the OPE through the main White House number, and an automated voice told me I could send a fax or leave a message. I did both, picking a name off the list of OPE people: Brian Bond, constituent liaison. His job description seemed closest to what I was looking for, and I felt like I needed someone named Bond, and Brian would do if James wasn't available.

I composed a letter, putting urgency into it, and faxed it through the college offices. When I returned to my room, Paul Grondahl called me back.

"What's up now?" he asked, and I told him.

Paul, who loves to shake up officialdom when he can, was very attentive while I vented at length in a way that might make my students' hair stand on end. I was not only tired, I was sore as hell about this, and I wasn't holding back in saying so. It was ridiculous, I said, how much it took to do this. Smugglers and pirates get animals through, and I can't help these guys?

"I'm staring out my window at the Rocky Mountains," I told him. "I think it would be easier to move them than to get this eagle here."

Paul, listening to my rant, took his notes, asked his questions, and signed off. As I closed my cell phone, I silently blessed him and all the others who took the time to care about this. I took a moment to be grateful for the help received thus far, though I was feeling pretty shaky about the prospects. What if it led nowhere? What if Mitch died in the meantime? What if I failed?

I was eight thousand feet up, deprived of oxygen and trying to make sure I did well in a new job. I was terribly worried about my husband as he went through the grief of losing a job he was really good at, and the frustrations of finding a new one. We were both incredibly stressed about our financial situation. I was still grieving the death of my mother. In spite of that, or maybe also because of that, I could not, I would not, ring the bell on Eagle Mitch. Greg and Scott, who went through much worse, hadn't done so. How could I?

I went back to my computer and started e-mailing my State Department contacts, other news outlets, Caroline Wekselbaum, and more.

CHAPTER 11

I Know I Can Count on You

Dear Ms. Smith:

Last month, my constituents Barbara Chepaitis and Pete Dubacher told me the incredible story of Navy SEALS stationed in Afghanistan who had rescued and were caring for a wounded Steppe Eagle. The SEALS sought the assistance of Mr. Dubacher of Berkshire Bird Paradise bird sanctuary in upstate New York to find a permanent home for this wounded bird. With the help of my office and the persistent efforts of Ms. Chepaitis and Mr. Dubacher, the Fish and Wildlife Service has issued an import permit and the Afghan Government has issued an export permit for the eagle.

Unfortunately, there is a ban on the import of avian species from Afghanistan, due to the threat of avian flu. My constituents are seeking a waiver of the ban for this particular bird. I would urge you to issue this waiver, after thoroughly evaluating the bird to ensure that it is disease-free . . . and poses no threat. . . . I strongly believe this bird merits special consideration based on the extraordinary circumstances surrounding his rescue by U.S. Navy SEALS. This unusual story has received media attention and serves as an inspirational reminder of the heroism of U.S. Armed Forces deployed around the world.

I know I can count on your cooperation in reviewing this matter and advising me of your findings as expeditiously as possible.

Sincerely,
Charles E. Schumer
United States Senator

That day in class my cell phone was once again on my desk. My class eyed it, then looked at me, concerned.

"How's it going with Mitch?" my student Julie asked.

"Not good," I said. I explained about the USDA and said I was waiting for some calls.

"Game over?" Barbara Caldwell asked.

"Not if I have anything to say about it," I answered grimly. "These institutions have their own rules, but that doesn't mean you back down. That's something you need to know as writers, because you'll be dealing with the publishing industry, which has even weirder rules." I bent their ears some more about dealing with institutions, and I hoped this would be useful to them in finding their own center of determination, something all writers need to own. While I was in the middle of it, my phone rang.

I looked down at it. The caller ID said the White House. I looked at my class. "I'd better take this," I said.

I don't know why, but everything in me said I had to stand at attention while speaking with the White House, so I stood up before I opened my phone and said hello. The voice on the other end asked, "Is this Barbara Che—Che—"

"Chepaitis," I said. "Yes, this is Barbara."

"This is Brian Bond, calling from the Office of Public Engagement," he said. "I understand you have a problem with an eagle."

Bond. Brian Bond. I actually teared up. Then I composed myself, and told him the story, my students watching closely, silently.

Later, my student Kyle would tell me he remembered how the tone of the class changed, becoming very serious, and how they all felt they were part of the seriousness, the struggle, because they saw my face, heard my voice. As writers they're incredibly observant of small gestures and their meaning, and Kimberly said I kept flipping my hair back, and that hair flip looked like I was saying "You'd better get this bird here or I'll kick your ass." She said she had no doubt that was somehow heard on the other end. Kelby said I held one arm out, ready for a fight.

I was. But I didn't need it here. Brian was carefully attentive, and he spoke with the courteous professionalism you would expect from the White House. He treated me like I mattered, like Mitch mattered, and he meant it. He also told me he would start working on it right away. He asked me to send an e-mail with the details. He would, he said, do whatever he could to help. I believed him.

When I hung up, for a moment all I could do was breathe, first with relief, and then with a tingling of excitement at possibilities opening up. I turned a grin to my class, resisting the urge to just laugh out loud. "That was the White House," I said. "They said they'll help."

I tried to say it casually, as if that sort of thing happened to me all the time. I was concerned about taking class time away from their writing, worried about doing my job well. This was a class about writing, not eagles, after all. But then, as I thought about it, I realized Eagle Mitch was also about writing, even then. My book about a bird sanctuary got me involved in the first place. And being an authentic human, delving deeply into your own soul and the complexities of being human, is one of the most important skills of the writer. Clearly Mitch demanded that of me, and had a lot to teach others about it.

"You never know where writing will lead you, right?" I said, and we talked about it. How writers trip through open doors out of curiosity or enthusiasm, only to find that something will be asked of them. They'll have to make choices, respond or not respond. And at all times they have to be ready to speak up, speak out. To howl. Being an advocate for an eagle or for your own work is the same skill set.

Kimberly told me later that she had always been phone-phobic, not even wanting to bother her best friend when she needed her. And there I was, bugging the White House about an eagle. It taught her something.

Discussion moved naturally from the difficulty of advocating for an eagle to the difficulty of getting published these days. Traditional publishers had narrowed their margins for what was acceptable, focusing a lot more on what has sold in the past rather than on work that's interesting. Everyone wanted a sure thing, within clearly delineated boundaries, and established writers as well as new ones had to push to get their work out there. My students were worried about this, and one of them, bemoaning his fate, said, "Man, I don't know if it even makes sense to try anymore."

When he said that, all that had just happened swirled itself into some kind of coherent whole, and I laughed. They looked a little surprised, so I laughed more, threw my hands up. "The White House just called me," I said. "The *White* House. About an *eagle*. If that can happen, what are you calling impossible?"

They thought about it, and they laughed, too.

"OWWUU," I howled. And they howled with me.

The phone call from Brian was just the beginning of the next leg of the journey, and there was lots more work to be done. After class, I sent out volumes of posts to the usual places. And I sent Brian an e-mail, thorough and formal, explaining what had happened with the USDA, and what I hoped would happen next.

"I am seeking your help in finding the appropriate auspices under which this eagle can come directly to the U.S., undergo its 30 day quarantine, and move on to the sanctuary," I wrote. "These young men did an admirable and compassionate thing in a very difficult situation in rescuing and caring for this bird, and I do not want it to die of red tape."

Brian was true to his word, and though I'll never know exactly what he did, I know he did something. Along with his work, a few more boats sailed into harbor. The article Paul Grondahl wrote was printed the next day and, much to my surprise, it showed up on the Internet in a lot of unexpected places and drew a great deal of comment.

One of its landing sites was Rachel Maddow's blog. She carried a photo of Mitch, and a copy of the article, headed with this commentary:

> Navy SEALs in Afghanistan rescued this eagle after it was shot by an Afghan soldier at a firing range. The SEALs have named the bird Mitch. They're trying to bring it back to the U.S., to a bird rescue center. The Albany Times-Union reports: "The USDA has a ban on any bird imported from Afghanistan due to fears of avian flu. USDA officials rebuffed Chepaitis' efforts to pay for testing and to agree to a mandatory quarantine period. They suggested shipping the bird to a foreign country that does not have an Afghan bird ban, waiting 90 days until the bird establishes residency and applying for an import permit from USDA."
>
> The story of the SEALs and their kindness toward Mitch is about the only bright spot in the war, at least that's visible from here. July has become the deadliest month for U.S. troops of the entire nine-year Operation Enduring Freedom. America has lost 66 troops this month, including six casualties announced Friday. June had been the grimmest so far, with 60 troops lost.

People responded to the story, posting questions, posting comments. "Emma Skeptic" asked why it was shot, and whether it was an accident or not, and "Leslie JK" responded that she had no doubt it was shot on purpose, and she hoped it would be placed where it wouldn't be used as target practice again. "Don Quixokie" was glad it could be saved; and proud that we were acting as goodwill ambassadors to nonhuman Afghans. His question: does it have legal visitor status, can it get a work permit, or does it have diplomatic protection?

"Dancinhrblady" was tearing up at the story, and said we've sent troops to a place they don't understand to do an impossible job, and they go ahead and knock themselves out to save an eagle. She was, she said, proud of them. But I suppose my favorite comment was from "Pixie-O," who said, "Gotta love oversight agencies. Can't test seafood for Corexit, but they can force a bird to get a Green Card."

I was encouraged that other people saw this as meaningful, and encouraged further when my e-mail to Brad Parker got some motion going as well. He'd been in touch with Greta Lundeberg, who had given us Dave Lawson's name. She e-mailed both me and Caroline, saying Brad had already reached out to "our USDA colleagues as well as the Embassy in Kabul" to see who might help there. He also spoke with the Afghan embassy in Washington, DC, which suggested that a letter from Senator Schumer's office would help speed things up in Afghanistan.

Senator Schumer wrote it, bless the man, because it worked, and the response was almost immediate.

Let me just say right here that I tend to be naive about issues of institutional power, which may be why Pluto felt it was necessary to round out my education in these matters, but after this I would understand, in a very personal way, how politics at its best is about service rather than personal gratification. How important it is to have someone willing to lift you up when you can't lift yourself.

So bless the senator, bless all those overworked people in the White House and the State Department who turned their thoughts toward a solution to this. Bless Dave Lawson and the WCS and Paul Grondahl and Rachel Maddow and Pixie-O and my supportive students and all the embassy people, and Caroline, and Scott and Greg as well.

Bless them all, because they gave a damn.

My next calls came from people at the USDA, asking me questions about Eagle Mitch, because they had heard from Senator Schumer and the White House and the State Department, and they were working to figure this out.

One call, from a USDA doctor whose name I don't remember, also came during class, and I'm sure I paced and flipped my hair even more as I spoke to him. He wanted to know if Pete Dubacher's facilities were adequate to care for this eagle, which made me laugh. When I used the word "aviary," he didn't know what it meant. And this was someone who got to decide where Mitch went?

I explained what an aviary is, and how Pete had been caring for eagles for thirty-five years, and how much Eagle Mitch's presence would mean to the thousands of visitors who got to hear his story, as well as to the young men who wanted him to have a safe home. The doctor listened, and said he would report back, and that they were all doing everything possible to make this happen.

Clearly, the USDA was on board and trying to get this right, but they had to go through their own process, and waiting for that to happen wasn't easy. Of course, I'm not someone who ever waits easily.

I paced. I flipped my hair. I talked on the phone. And while I waited, I wrote.

CHAPTER 12

Almost Impossible

Facebook status update:

Chepaitis: Did you know it's almost impossible to ship frozen rats to Afghanistan?

Misfit Pete: That is probably the only time ever, in the history of the universe, that anyone has written that particular sentence.

A few days later, when I was done with my summer teaching session and back home from Colorado, I got word that the USDA had given us a temporary waiver of the ban on import of birds from Afghanistan. This time my happy dance was in the office of my own home, alone. But it was very happy indeed.

When I called Paul Grondahl to let him know and to thank him for his article, he said, "I figured it was okay, because USDA public relations has been calling me." They wanted to make sure everyone knew they were working for this, and Paul's voice mattered to them. Huh. Another lesson brought home: never underestimate the power of the press.

However, USDA permission still hinged on Mitch's having a negative avian flu test, and going through a fifteen-day quarantine in Afghanistan that was up to USDA standards. That was no simple matter. In fact, nothing was simple in Afghanistan. Nothing at all.

By now it was August and we had been at this Eagle Mitch thing since the end of June, but it seemed solving the USDA issue simply created more work to be done. I wasn't getting any more rest than I had in Colorado, though I had a lot more oxygen available. Throughout that month I kept wondering how many e-mails it would take to save an eagle. The quick answer was a lot.

E-mails flew between me and the USDA and Greg and Scott and Caroline, with lots of new and unfamiliar names attached, people who, in ways large or small, were supporting this effort. One of my most memorable days was when I got a call from a woman at the USDA named Bambi. I thought it was a joke at first. A woman named Bambi, calling about Eagle Mitch? What were the odds?

As it turned out she was very real, and she was calling with encouragement, and suggestions about how to get food to Mitch. She was a lovely woman, and I was very happy to hear from her. However, neither she nor I could do anything about the rest of the work that had to be accomplished before we got Mitch here. Most of it had to happen in Afghanistan.

Crates for quarantine and travel had to be made or found, food had to be obtained, travel and paperwork logistics figured out. The guys, in between their military duties, had to get transport for Mitch to see a veterinarian—a six-hour flight from base camp—and the veterinarian had to deem him fit for quarantine, get hold of an avian flu test, and administer it right before quarantine, which would constitute another transport issue. Just arranging that with Greg's and Dr. Jenkins's schedules took weeks.

By this time Greg was doing most of the care for Mitch, Scott's duties having taken him elsewhere. His daily routine would include waking up a little earlier in the morning, going to Mitch's cage and opening it, then throwing a towel over him because Mitch would stay calm that way.

At first, he would just let Mitch out to run around on a big concrete pad near the cage, but he was cutting his feet up on the gravel, which was bad for the bumblefoot problem, so Greg built a perch for him out of scrap wood and started putting him on that instead. From his perch Mitch could stretch his wings and hop about, getting much-needed exercise while Greg cleaned out his cage and changed his water.

Every other day or so they would get a live chicken from the mess hall and put it in his cage. Before camp got too busy or the day got too hot Greg would approach Mitch, who would jump off the perch and run to the corner of the pad and corner himself. Greg would put him back under his towel and get him back into his cage, where he could feast on his chicken. At night he would return to check on him and give him more food.

They were trying to feed him as much as possible, getting him ready for his big journey, but he stayed underweight. It seemed he was missing something vital that he could only get through his more natural diet of rodents, some important nutrients found only in rat guts and bones. Here in the United States, Pete Dubacher had lots of frozen rats for his eagles—ratsicles, we call them—and we were more than willing to send Mitch a steady supply, but nobody at Federal Express, the U.S. Post Office, or UPS would ship them to Afghanistan. There was the issue of using dry ice, and the issue of exporting and then importing dead animals, which required a twisted and tortuous routine of paperwork. On the Afghanistan end there was also the issue of where to ship them, since everyone involved was in a different location, and some of them didn't have addresses that UPS would ship to. Even if they did, in all likelihood the rats would be confiscated on arrival. It would take longer and would be more difficult to ship the ratsicles than to get Mitch home.

Instead, my husband found a place that sold dried raptor food. The food itself was pretty inexpensive, but shipping it would cost two hundred dollars. When I called UPS to see if we could get a discount, they said no. They went on to name all the "important" charities they contributed to, and it was clear we weren't one of them.

It didn't matter. We sent the food.

While all that was happening, the mobius strip of paperwork continued to slowly unwind, and my patience with it often gave out. Once or twice, it gave out on Eileen Jenkins, the army veterinarian who would care for Mitch through his flu tests and Afghanistan quarantine process. Though I grew to appreciate everything about her, our initial e-mail interactions were a little testy. This was because she had the unfortunate job of telling us that Mitch was not fit for quarantine. Not at all.

She and veterinarian Jim McCord concurred on this. Mitch was too thin, and his wounds were infected, and he just wasn't up to it. They were putting him on medication, which Greg and Scott would have to administer. They'd adjust his cage slightly, and try to deal with the wounds and bumblefoot as well. In two weeks they would re-examine him, and then they would have a better idea of prognosis and timeline.

Two weeks? Two weeks, and all we would get was a possible prognosis? But the guys were getting closer and closer to going home, and this bird needed to be out of a war zone, and I didn't understand what was so rough about quarantine, or how it could be worse than where he was now.

I wrote back, whining as professionally as I could, and she was good enough not to call me an idiot, though I'm guessing she thought it. Nor would I blame her. Instead, she said that trying to rehabilitate a raptor in a war zone was full of challenges. And she called me "ma'am."

Stuck waiting, I had to at least squeak my wheels. I wrote back to her:

> Dr. Jenkins,
> Thank you for your information regarding Eagle Mitch's physical exam and the resulting delay in his quarantine and transport to the U.S. You mention that rehabilitating a raptor in a war zone is full of challenges, but I've known this since Craig and Scott sought our help. I've been working very hard to get Mitch to safe haven and relieve Craig and Scott of the burden of care. And believe me, much of what I've encountered has seemed designed specifically to thwart us. We've gotten this far only through the conscientious efforts of many people to overcome a variety of obstacles.
> I have said from the beginning that I don't want Mitch to die of red tape, because clearly each delay has led to a

deterioration in his condition, decreasing the likelihood that we'll complete the simple act of saving this eagle.

While I appreciate that we don't want to put Mitch at risk by moving him if he isn't up to it, I wonder if there isn't some way to get him into a situation that improves his odds for recovery. Would he have better care available if he was in USDA quarantine? I don't know what a USDA quarantine situation is, so perhaps you could explain that to me. If that isn't the case, is there anything else that can be done to help Craig and Scott with his care?

The best solution, as you pointed out, is to get Mitch out of the war zone, and any thoughts you have on removing impediments to his transport would be greatly appreciated by all concerned. As usual, if I can be of any help, I'll gladly do so.

Eileen e-mailed back, to explain more fully:

I'm not sure if you're aware, but Mitch is in one location, CPT Reaves is in another, and I am at still another. Travel in Afghanistan is dangerous and requires significant logistical support. Mitch will have to be moved into quarantine at either CPT Reaves' location or mine. Though he's been in a cage by himself since his rescue, a key element of quarantine is daily observation by trained veterinary personnel and that has not, and cannot, happen at Mitch's current location.

I hope you can appreciate that we are doing EVERY-THING we can, but it takes HUGE effort here. Neither CPT Reaves' clinic nor my clinic is set up for raptor quarantine, and I am the only staff member trained to handle raptors, so we have huge hurdles to overcome just to keep him IN quarantine. We also have the issues associated with U.S. importation requirements such as testing for Highly Pathogenic Avian Influenza and Exotic New Castle Disease (both endemic here).

I'm telling you all these things so that you are aware of the challenges we face, and so perhaps you can understand what we are doing and why. The list of issues above is only a partial one. We are working diligently to find ways to resolve all the issues quickly, as we all leave in less than 45 days.

I grumbled myself into a less petulant state as I began to understand her plight, but I still wasn't happy. Every delay seemed to lessen the prospects for Mitch, and now each one also created issues of coordinating paperwork and testing with USDA requirements, which would quickly burgeon into a logistical nightmare. Already some of the e-mails I was getting had scheduling outlines that were totally incomprehensible to me. Just trying to read them felt like chewing on aluminum foil.

But to everyone's credit, not once did any of them suggest giving up or bowing out. We all wanted to get this done by now. Once in a while we would even get a bit of good news, though even that had its gruesome side.

One day, Greg and a buddy were driving back from chow hall and what he thought at first was one of the local wild dogs ran out in front of them. They hit it hard, and when they got out to look, they saw it was a fox, too far gone to be saved. After they put it out of its misery it occurred to Greg that it would make a perfect meal for Mitch, so they skinned it, brought it to him, and put it in his cage.

"The next day the carcass was down to mostly bones," Greg wrote to me. "I guess he liked it!"

He had also found a source for a few mice from a lab, so Mitch was getting some of the rodents he needed, and his medication seemed to be working. Over the next two weeks he gained weight, and his wounds began to heal. Greg thought he was looking good to be approved for quarantine. Then he would be given his flu tests, which were being flown in specially just for him.

I would say I was cautiously hopeful, but there's nothing cautious about hope. And with Mitch I had found that every point of progress was also another opportunity for crisis.

The next one would be have to be fielded by Dr. Eileen Jenkins.

CHAPTER 13

The Smell of Hearts and Brains

Dear Caroline and Bettina,

If you read these emails from the bottom up, you'll see that the Avian flu test thawed in transit, and Major Jenkins doesn't know how long it will be before another arrives. Also note that Craig is leaving in 30 days, so time is not on our side.

I'm pleading with you to see if there's any way to expedite this process. Can Mitch go into USDA quarantine now and get the test done while there, as Craig suggests? Anything that you can do would be greatly appreciated.

Cordially,
Barbara Chepaitis

Eileen said that when the avian flu test arrived at her office, her biggest mistake was opening the box.

When she did, the smell almost overwhelmed her. It was, she said, awful. Horrendous. Sickening. The kind of smell that makes you run to the bathroom to retch.

The test itself is made from hearts and brains—an interesting metaphor when you think of Etana's eagle and serpent, but not so interesting when you open a boxful that have been rotting in transit for some days.

Then, even more sickening was the realization that this test, which took so long to get, was no good.

Greg responded with his usual understatement. "Bummer," he said, "But I suppose these things happen. On the upside, Mitch is doing well. And Captain Reaves said the University here could donate ten mice, so we'll pick those up shortly." He gave some suggestions for solutions, some ways that might make it possible to go ahead in spite of the current disaster. He was taking the news much better than I was.

Well, maybe he knew something I didn't. Or maybe he just trusted that Eileen, army-trained to be resourceful, would figure something out.

She did.

Like the two young men involved with Mitch, Eileen is a quietly remarkable woman. My interactions with her during the Mitch saga, like my interactions with Greg and Scott, were all about getting this bird home, but I spoke with her at more leisure when she was back in the United States.

At that time she was three months away from her eleven-year wedding anniversary, though she and her husband, also in the army, calculated they'd only lived together for a total of three years. They laughed about what it would be like to actually spend an entire year in the same house, something they were looking forward to as they moved to a new post, this time together.

Eileen, raised in a military family, went into the army understanding the drawbacks, but she liked the sense of larger purpose service brought, the sense of belonging to something bigger than she was. And she also had a lifelong love of animals.

When she was three years old she told her mother she was going to be a veterinarian. When she was six and her cat trapped a mouse in a stone wall she took her beach pail and rescued it. Thrilled with her victory, she brought her pail full of mouse to her mother, who maybe wasn't so thrilled but who encouraged her daughter anyway.

"She told me to always be wary of anyone who mistreats animals or children," Eileen said. "She understood what that meant."

Eileen went on to hold jobs as an EMT, and she went to nursing school, but she found she loved animal medicine best. Animals are more vulnerable, and for her, the practice was more pure than human medicine, without the restrictions insurance companies and big business create in that realm. She got her veterinary degree while in the army, and when it came time to focus her practice she did internships in zoo medicine, wildlife medicine, a decision that would later serve Mitch well. She ended up in Afghanistan because veterinary personnel are in high demand there, and deployed regularly. Her job was to care for military working dogs, to contract working dogs for the United States and its allies, and to make sure the food supply was safe. She found all her duties to be amazing work, as fulfilling as she always imagined animal medicine would be.

The military dogs she cared for—yes, the ones that worked to capture bin Laden—literally save lives on a daily basis. They're trained to sniff out old Russian mines and IEDs, to parachute into remote areas with their humans, to go into tricky situations ahead of their human units, following commands through a remote-control collar. Each one is worth thousands of dollars, as well as an incalculable amount in the companionship they provide to their human coworkers.

At the bottom of her e-mails, Eileen includes a quote from General David Petraeus about these animals: "The capability military working dogs bring to the fight cannot be replicated by man or machine. By all measures of performance, their yield outperforms any asset we have in our inventory." Caring for these intelligent and loving creatures was, for Eileen, a wonderful privilege.

The rest of her job entailed work with animal husbandry, something that has a large impact on a country where the land can be harsh, and food sources scarce. "One of the big problems in Afghanistan is lack of protein sources," she told me, "so the more we ensure that farm animals are healthy, the more we empower the people to prosper, and that's what makes them truly independent. That, and education."

Like Greg and Scott, she was both astonished by the beauty of the country and its people, and saddened by what they had to contend with. "The life expectancy there is forty-four years of age, the literacy rate is 33 percent, and the infant mortality rate is huge," she told me. "But the spectacular mountains, the incredible history here—it's so beautiful. And the people, well, they're just people. They want to raise their families, be safe, practice their religion. There are evil people here, just like anywhere, but there's amazing people, too."

There was one village she visited regularly to train veterinary students, local butchers, and farmers, and every time she showed up one of the village elders would bring her chai tea in a clear glass cup. "Sugar's very expensive here, very hard to get," she said, "but he'd hand me my cup and you could see a half-inch of sugar still on the bottom. He was saying, 'I can do this for you, and I want to.' And it was a sacrifice for him, but it was his gift of hospitality—something that's really important here."

Eileen felt good about the work she did there, teaching people how to preserve their meat and deworm their livestock so every bit of food they gave the animal counted. And teaching them how to link all this together, too, was a way of jumping a people forward six hundred years. What she and others like her were doing made a difference.

When we hear about Afghanistan in the news, it's generally about violence, bombs exploding, terrorist action and U.S. military reaction. It doesn't occur to us that many of the people in service there are taking care of goats, or working with dogs to get rid of land mines. While I'll admit freely that I was very much against President Bush's decision to invade Iraq, I'll also say that I'm for the kind of work Eileen is doing, and I admire the courage required for anyone to take on the kind of service Scott and Greg chose. In a perfect world, of course I would prefer they didn't have to be there, but we all know the world is far from perfect. However, there are many people who go into service to try and get it a little closer to the mark. I was glad to meet some of them, thoughtful young people who wanted to make a difference, and were clearly doing so.

While the saga of Eagle Mitch was unfolding I would regularly go to the little country convenience story near my house to get copies of newspapers that carried the story. The owners were from Pakistan, and one of the men working there, Sayed, was from Afghanistan.

"All these newspapers," he said. "You must like to read."

I laughed and explained that I was writer, explained about Eagle Mitch. He called the owner over and made him listen to the story again, and they were intrigued, asked lots of questions. I told them what Greg and Scott and Eileen said about the country, and their emphasis on the need for education. Scott told me that one day, as he was working with a group of about a hundred Afghan soldiers in training, he asked how many of them could read. Out of a hundred, only twelve raised their hands.

"Yes," Sayed agreed. "Exactly. But it will change. It is changing. You know, the generation born after the war with Russia, they were hungry for blood. The ones born in the next generation were hungry for things. Now, this generation is hungry for learning."

Eileen already knew that, but with Eagle Mitch, she had a whole new set of skills to learn herself, a whole new set of problems to deal with.

When the avian flu test arrived in her office ruined, she knew how hard it would be to get another test in time for this eagle to survive. And there were no guarantees a second test wouldn't arrive in the same condition. She was devastated.

By then she was attached to the bird, and to the young men who were caring for him. Not that long ago she had actually found another injured Steppe Eagle on the airstrip of Bagram Airfield, where she went running every morning. That bird was hardly moving at all, and had obviously been there suffering for a long time. Though she had to get special clearance to retrieve it, she went to the trouble only to find that it was too far gone for her to save. To her sorrow, it had to be euthanized.

When Eagle Mitch came to her he was in better condition but still very close to the edge. "He was so skinny, I had no idea how he was alive, except that Scott and Greg were so resourceful in helping him," she said. "The size of their hearts and compassion was all that determined how well he did, even though they were up against such awful odds."

And she remembered how Greg's eyes lit up when it was clear Mitch was getting well. She couldn't let a spoiled avian flu test ruin that. She had to figure this out, for them as well as this bird.

What she did next makes her one of My Heroes. She decided that if she couldn't get a test, she would just have to make one.

She found out what raw ingredients were needed, got information on the right formula for using them, and located a source in Germany to have what she needed shipped to her. Like Greg and Scott and Bettina Cooper, she isn't one to brag, so I didn't know this until it was well over—which may be a good thing, given how twitchy I was already. But it seemed every solution with Mitch led only to another problem, especially in a country where travel was both difficult and high-risk.

"The distance between places isn't that far, but Afghanistan is unique," she said. "It's not like Iraq, where there's cities and roads and buildings. That didn't exist where we were. And there's still plenty of people who want to kill us. You can't just get in a car and go."

As she figured out how to make the test, she also had to figure out how to get something that's almost nonexistent in Afghanistan: dry ice. "That's where good luck, or synchronicity or coincidence if you prefer, found us," she said. "I had a friend working in the blood transport unit, and I found out that their commander was an old roommate of mine. They were the only unit like that in Afghanistan. And they had dry ice. It was perfect." They got some for her, and she had the ingredients shipped to her and made her test.

At the same time, she had to figure out how to build a regulation quarantine crate for Mitch, in a country where materials are hard to come by. Her go-to guy, Sergeant Mike Dezellum, helped her figure that out, and supplies arrived from all the people in the area who had become interested in Mitch, those who met him or heard his story and wanted to help.

Some of those people happened to work in pest control, their job to put out poison to kill rodents. When they heard about Mitch, they put out live traps as well, and brought their catch to Eileen. She would quarantine the rodents, euthanize them, freeze them, and feed them to Mitch.

Ah! Ratsicles. Home grown.

Mitch was with her near Bagram Airfield for six or seven weeks, and though he was stressed at first, banging himself up a lot, once he calmed down he learned to trust the people he lived with. Eileen or Mike could walk right up to him and he would stay calm, knowing they were the creatures who brought the ratsicles. People who made good things happen.

During that time Eileen continued to be heartened by all the offers of help, the signs of compassionate humanity Mitch's situation brought out in those who met him. It made her begin to think that Mitch himself was a bird with a mission, "like he had something he had to accomplish, too. And he wasn't about to give up on his job either."

Given my interactions with birds, I wouldn't be at all surprised.

Maybe he had to give a bunch of people in a war zone an opportunity to demonstrate their compassion, knowing that doing so keeps our hearts and souls alive. Maybe he had to give a stubborn, grieving woman in the United States the chance to try and make one thing come out right in a year when everything seemed wrong. Maybe he had to come here, carrying with him the stories of the land he came from and its people, along with those visitors who were working to help them.

Poet Joy Harjo wrote about a vision she had of traveling far above the earth and viewing it from that perspective:

> This beloved planet we call home was covered with an elastic web of light. I watched in awe as it shimmered, stretched, dimmed and shined, shaped by the collective effort of all life within it. . . . .The most humble kindness made the brightest light. Nothing was wasted. (*The Woman Who Fell from the Sky*, p. 10)

The humble kindness of caring for a wounded bird was shimmering in widening circles, moving out from Mitch to all the people he met, and all the people they told the story to, and more. If Mitch survived, he would go to a place where his story would be told to thousands of schoolchildren, all of them learning that heroes aren't always about guns. Sometimes, heroes are about healing. About kindness.

If you believe in such things, you might say Mitch knew exactly where he needed to go, and made sure that all the necessary humans were available to get him there.

If they could complete the job, that is. One piece of it was completed in September: Eileen administered Mitch's flu tests and put him in quarantine. Now all we had to do was wait.

As if that were the easy part.

CHAPTER 14

One Negative Test—Ready to Proceed

Hello All,
    I sent you both an earlier email about a possible second test . . . we are going to proceed with the 1 negative test. We will do follow up on Mitch in the NYAIC. . . .
Let's move forward!!!!!

Bettina T. Cooper DVM MPH
Avian Import Specialist/VMO

By September my husband still hadn't found a job, but he was doing consultancy work, bringing in money, and that made him feel a whole lot better. He celebrated by doing something he loves—driving really fast.

His motto is that any day you get to squeak a wheel is a good day, something he meant a little differently than I did. But I liked seeing him happy, so I was glad when he found kart racing, a way to get back out on the track that we could afford. I even agreed to go with him, and to take a half day of instruction in driving kart. Once I took the course, I would be let loose on the racetrack with a bunch of adolescent boys out to discharge some testosterone. It was fun, and it was also a lot harder than I thought it would be, but what I remember best about it is the instructor telling us how to manage when there was a crash on the track.

"You see a wreck ahead of you, don't look at it," he told us. "Keep your eye on where you want to go, on your racing line. You'll naturally move toward what you look at, so look at where you want to go."

That, I think, is what I did while I was waiting for the avian flu test results. I didn't dare look at the potential wreck ahead of me. Instead, I kept my eye on where I wanted to go. Where I wanted Eagle Mitch to go. I kept any fear strictly out of my line of vision.

I was pretty busy, anyway, running new classes online for my graduate students, finishing up some other writing projects, and looking into transport possibilities for Mitch. Greg said he might be able to bring him home when he came back if the timing worked out, but just in case I was exploring other airlines from Afghanistan to the United States. And if Mitch did take a military flight, I would still have to get him from Greg's landing point in Virginia to his New York State quarantine in Newburgh.

I kept my vision on all that, my current racing line, and tried not to think of what would happen if Mitch's test was no good. I reminded myself that I had no control over that, and Pluto was trying to teach me the difference between using my power for what I could control and ignoring what I could. If, now and then, I felt a hot sweat creeping up the back of my neck about it, I would just go back to work, writing another Eagle Mitch post, speaking with another journalist, working on transport.

It wasn't until I got the e-mail from Dr. Cooper, from the USDA, telling me that Mitch was negative and good to go that I allowed myself to feel how scared I had really been. Instead of e-mailing her back, I picked up the phone and dialed her number.

"Bettina?" I said when I heard her voice on the other end. "The test is negative?" I hadn't said who I was, and I was using her first name for the first time, speaking to her like a friend.

On the other end, her soft, kind voice replied, hesitant and surprised. "Ms. Chepaitis?" she asked.

"That's right," I said. "I had to hear you say it. Mitch is okay?"

She laughed, and assured me he was. And she seemed just as thrilled as I was. We went over some of the tasks still ahead of us, but

I didn't hear much of it, because the party in my head was drowning a lot out.

"Thank you," I said to her. "Thank you so much."

We shared something now. She worked hard for this, and in many ways her job was more difficult than mine. I only had to be a thorn in everyone's side, including hers. She had to deal with my impatience, my penchant for calling newspapers and senators, *and* the strict regulations of an enormous institution that had her job in its keeping. More than once as we worked through paperwork details, she stopped and said she had to clear whatever it was with her higher-ups. Sometimes she would sigh, "We'll have to have a meeting about that." Though my main concern was Mitch, I also felt for her. Meetings. Brrrr.

In spite of pressure, she was consistently calm, and apparently she could negotiate the complex paperwork that made my hair stand on end. To my mind, she was becoming a model of what a regular worker within a mammoth institution can do to make the system work for the people it's supposed to serve. After the last year's experience I was pretty cynical about that possibility. Institutions like my mother's nursing home and Social Security, which began as systems meant to serve people's needs, now seemed to exist only to serve themselves, their CEOs, and their profit margins. Bettina was showing me that it is possible to shift that, though it takes a good deal of effort.

My sister, who works for the health department, is another such role model. Her job concerns Medicaid and managed health systems, to my mind some of the most difficult stuff to deal with these days. Lately she's been dealing with a man whose daughter has Huntington's disease. She got stuck between old rules and new, and was in danger of not being able to continue seeing the doctor who had been treating her for some time, a doctor she trusted. My sister could have told this man that nothing could be done—very sorry, but no way, no how. Instead she worked to get him what he needed, and continues to do so. Beyond that, she's always willing to spend some time talking to him. That's a far cry from those who don't talk to people, and just do paper.

Senator Schumer's office was another example of that, and since his letter was a big part of making the shift possible, after I spoke to Dr. Cooper my next task was to send an e-mail to Caroline Wekselbaum, celebrating the good news with her. I also let her know I would be notifying the press. If she wanted me to do so through her office, that would be fine with me. She called and we sort of said "Yay" at each other for a while, and then got down to business. Yes, she said, the senator's office would put out a press release, and would I go over it with them?

"Anything," I said, thinking she could probably see me beaming from her New York City office. "Anything at all."

So, for the rest of that day and a good bit of that evening I consulted with Max Young in Senator Schumer's press office on the story, a task that felt pretty damn good. The final version Max sent out looked like this:

MITCH THE EAGLE COMING TO NEW YORK AFTER BEING RESCUED BY NAVY SEALS IN AFGHANISTAN— SCHUMER CUT THROUGH RED TAPE TO ENSURE EAGLES' PASSAGE BACK TO U.S.

Navy Seals, Stationed in Afghanistan, Rescued And Cared for Mitch the Eagle after He was Harmed

Barbara Chepaitis, Author and Advocate, and Schumer Cut Through Red Tape to Secure Safe Passage to America for Mitch

Schumer Weighed in With Personal Letter and Helped Secure Exemption to Blanket Ban on Imported Birds

Today, U.S. Senator Charles E. Schumer announced that Mitch, an eagle rescued and cared for by Navy Seals in Afghanistan, is on his way to a bird sanctuary in the Capital Region. After rescuing Mitch, a Steppe Eagle, the Navy Seals contacted Pete Dubacher, owner of Berkshire Bird Paradise in Petersburg NY, seeking his help. Barbara Chepaitis, author of Feathers of Hope, a book about the bird sanctuary, immediately went to Senator Schumer's office in an effort to secure Mitch's passage to the United States.

"We hit some serious obstacles while trying to help these young men rescue their eagle, but I knew Senator Schumer would support their efforts," Ms. Chepaitis said. "We absolutely could not have done this without him."

Schumer was able to cut through the red tape and expedite Fish and Wildlife paperwork along with the necessary health testing for Mitch with the U.S. Department of Agriculture (USDA), so the eagle can transition to a permanent home at Berkshire Bird Paradise. He will arrive in the United States the first week in October.

"This is a great story about our caring soldiers and generous New Yorkers, I was happy to help give this effort a last boost and get Mitch here," Schumer said. "Some regulations at the USDA almost held this up but at the end of the day we were able to cut through the red tape and give Mitch a home right here in our backyard."

During a routine patrol, the Navy Seals saw Mitch being shot on a rifle range. The Seals were able to rescue the eagle and tend its wounds, ensuring its survival. The service members cared for this Steppe Eagle, whom they named "Mitch," building him a cage and feeding him as he healed. They soon discovered that Mitch's wing was permanently disabled, and through some research learned about the Berkshire Bird Paradise in Petersburg NY where director Pete Dubacher offers haven to birds from around the world, including many permanently injured eagles.

"I was in service during the Vietnam war," Dubacher said, "and I started rescuing birds at that time, so I know how tough it is for these young men to do what they did. Senator Schumer really stepped up to the plate for them, and for Mitch. As a veteran, I can't thank him enough."

A current ban on the import of avian species from Afghanistan due to threat of Avian flu almost prevented the possibility of bringing Mitch to safe haven. Schumer, through a personal letter, made it possible for Mitch to receive a one-time exemption once it was assured that he was disease-free.

"Of course, we all want to preserve the health laws, but we also knew that Mitch was a special case, destined for a sanctuary rather than public market. Senator Schumer's letter made that clear, which meant those at the USDA who wanted to help were able to move forward," Ms. Chepaitis said. "Everyone involved is very excited at being able to see this to a happy conclusion."

Mitch is currently slated to come to the U.S. the first week in October, where he will undergo precautionary tests until he is transferred to the Berkshire Bird Paradise, where the thousands of schoolchildren who visit every year will have the opportunity to hear a very special story, of a very special eagle.

I was pleased with the results, and so was Max. He was even more pleased when the Associated Press picked it up, though that meant little to me.

When I was getting my coffee the next morning and my husband was already tucked into his office, on his computer, I heard him exclaim, "Holy shit!"

"What?" I shot back. The last time he did that it turned out our cat was having a conversation with a porcupine on the front porch, so I expected something a little scary.

"Eagle Mitch," he said. "It's all over the place."

I went into his office and tracked the Google hits of the story. It was, well, everywhere. I read the story over and over, and over and over again. And each time I read it, I was surprised to see it, happy to see it, and more than a little miffed.

Miffed, because the final version, after AP did a slice and dice on it, read like this:

> 9/22   PETERSBURG, N.Y.—An eagle wounded on a firing range in Afghanistan and rescued by Navy SEALs is getting a new home at a bird sanctuary in upstate New York.
>
> Democratic Sen. Charles Schumer says federal officials agreed to let Mitch the Eagle into the U.S. despite a ban on importing birds from Afghanistan because of avian flu fears. Mitch will get to America in early October and undergo tests

before being sent to the Berkshire Bird Paradise in Petersburg, about 20 miles east of Albany.

The steppe eagle was shot in a wing by an Afghan soldier
at a training base in the southern part of the country. SEALs
on patrol saw the shooting and tended to Mitch's wounds.

Schumer said Wednesday the SEALs appealed for help
from the sanctuary, which contacted him.

There you go. All that work compacted down to a few para-
graphs that didn't mention my name. I could just hear a reporter saying, "Who's this? Barbara Che—Che—? Cut it."

"Good thing I didn't do it for the glory," I mentioned wryly. And
at least, I thought, Berkshire Bird Paradise got a mention. Pete kept his
eagles in ratsicles entirely through donation, so that was important.

If I was surprised, and even a little impressed, at the way the
AP can compress a full and rich story into a sound bite, I was more
surprised at the kind of reaction it garnered from readers.

The Huffington Post, which carried the story, had lots of comments on it, and they were strangely mixed. Some complained that
we were "wasting" resources on saving an eagle. We should, they said,
be out saving children. One person asked, "Why the F is this news?"

And a comment that made me scratch my head and wonder
said, "If you really want to help an animal go to your local animal
control. . . . how about saving them first! they are American BORN."

Okay, then.

Aside from some comical comments suggesting that Mitch was
probably a terrorist—at least, I think they were meant to be funny—an
interesting discussion developed after that. Someone with the screen
name of "HHUA" shot back at the complainers, "Why don't you folks
tell these guys directly how ashamed they should be of themselves for
engaging in an 'act of kindness' that helped boost their morale (while
living in conditions that could send them home in a box at any moment!) How DARE they be kind to a bird . . . I guess compassion is
OFF the table . . . since you have some bizarre belief that anyone who
is kind to a bird must somehow have a limit to their kindness that
would preclude humans."

There was more back and forth: people who saw saving an eagle as precluding other good deeds, people who said that any good deed makes more good things happen, people who said it was a political move and flag waving, people who said taking action was good and asked how many children the complainers had saved. I chimed in and said that getting the USDA to do this for us gave me hope. If that could happen, what else might be possible? So find something good to do, and go do it.

When someone commented, "Don't take this the wrong way, but you are a very attractive woman," I backed out of the discussion. I figured it had run its course. But I was glad for the talk. I figured it was just one more part of Eagle Mitch's mission. And I hoped then, as I hope now, that what I was able to do could be a model for others who were struggling to do their one good deed in this difficult and often wicked world. I believe that whether you're saving a child or a bird or a river or some other piece of shining goodness in the world, the principles are the same: Dig in, and keep going. Don't take "no" as the final answer. Don't ask yourself if something *can* be done. Instead ask how it *will* be done.

For that, you often have to go outside your own comfort zone in seeking help, and you have to be ready to generate creative solutions to the problems you confront, but if I can do it, so can you. That's one of the messages I wanted Eagle Mitch to spread. One of the skills I hoped our experience taught others.

I believe in teaching. If you remember my mother, you know I come by it honestly.

I felt hopeful as I watched the news stories unfold. As Max knew it would, the AP story generated a flurry of calls from other journalists in both news and television, and local press were already lining up for the big day of Mitch's arrival.

My hope, however, was tempered by a good deal of trepidation. I still carried the burden of many failed bird rescue attempts, and even while I celebrated the latest victory, I waited for the next set of obstacles that would surely come our way.

In this, I wasn't disappointed.

CHAPTER 15

First Port of Entry

Dear Eagle Mitch Friends,

It is with a mixture of joy, and sadness that I write this final (?) email to you all about Mitch. His departure date from Afghanistan is approaching, Oct. 1 with his U.S. arrival on Sunday, Oct. 3, first port of entry, Norfolk Naval Base in Virginia. . . .

I thank each of you for your detailed contribution to these plans. It was a long road, with a very resilient patient. There was a lot of heart that went into this very special animal—starting with the brave men that thought to befriend an animal they found under the worst conditions, and with such personal risk. That risk continued with each transport, with each foray for food, and only you all know the details of what you had to do.

Those of us that are Stateside can only admire your determination to see this animal out of harm's way and do our part.

So with this last email, I think our work is done. Above all, Greg, you and your men should feel a great sense of accomplishment. It's been great working with all of you.

Sincerely,
Dr. Bettina Cooper

Dr. Cooper's e-mail ended one important leg of the journey, but it was way too optimistic in thinking our work was done. In between her kind words were all the items that had to be attended to next. As I had learned from the Myth of Etana, high-flying idealism is worth little if it isn't grounded in persistent action on some very tedious details.

Just to give you a sense of how tedious those details were, here's her list of what needed to be done for officialdom. Feel free to skip it if your head starts hurting. Lord knows mine did:

1. Import permit- issued- Jenkins. Taylor, Craig White should have copies. . . . Jenkins will attach her original to outside of carrier (we realize you do not have a color printer- so Dr. Taylor- given the situation- please alert port vet to this discrepancy)

2. Health certificate- issued by Dr. Jenkins- attached to carrier

3. CITES- attached to outside of carrier

4. 17-8, including NVSL lab results- attached to outside of carrier, includes seal numbers (can be on Dr. Jenkins' own official form). She will determine how many to give to Craig White for breakage in flight-(for the purpose of maintenance of bird)

Any changes to hangar arrival- Greg will contact Port vet directly via blackberry - Dr. Karen Y. Floyd

1. Port vet meet plane- inspection, paperwork review, unseal and re-seal . . . allowing hour rest before re-seal

2. Port Vet disinfect immediate area housing carrier and associated bird debris- removal of bird waste for incineration, etc. (per SOP)

3. Dr. Taylor will coordinate USFWS inspection or will coordinate their needs with the plane arrival

4. 1 hour food and rest stop upon deplaning.

Travel to New York Animal Import Center

1. Ms. Chepaitis- I cannot find the name of the company from your previous emails, that will be taking Mitch to the quarantine facility. Can you please respond to this email by letting the group know the name of the company you are using to move Mitch? Mitch must remain sealed and an approximate time called into the quarantine station so they will know when to expect him. This is part of an official transport, and until Mitch clears his second quarantine stay, his health status is still questionable. Please make the driver understand any unauthorized stops will have negative consequences.

2. The driver should submit all paperwork issued by the Port veterinarian in Va. to the NYAIC- Dr. Davis.

NYAIC - 30 days quarantine- as per CFR regulations

Clearly, there were still a lot of boxes to be checked.

In the meantime, we were all nervous about the flight to the States. Greg would be taking Mitch on a military plane, and that was good, but it also had some scary parts. Bad things can happen on military flights, and Greg would have to stop along the way in places that might not appreciate Mitch's story. Eileen Jenkins knew better than I did the risks the journey would entail.

Though Mitch had passed his avian flu test, he had to go directly from Afghanistan into U.S. quarantine. He would have to travel under strict quarantine conditions, which meant Eileen had to ensure his crate allowed no other birds to interact with him and no rodents to get to him, but he still needed ventilation en route. She told me, "Then, I thought, oh my God, what if they stop in Germany? They could just say 'We're killing this bird.' We all kept telling Greg, 'Dude, whatever you do, don't leave the base with the bird because as long as you're on base you're on American soil.'"

To use Greg's talent for understatement, we were all a little tense. What we had going for us was that Greg had already traveled around Afghanistan with Mitch, taking him from one veterinarian to another, one official to another, as he got all the boxes checked off on his paperwork trail. Mitch, he said, traveled well, going through six-hour flights with no trouble. At first Mitch would be agitated, and Greg had to take care that he didn't injure himself, but once Mitch's crate was covered and the flight began, he settled down and slept, undisturbed by takeoff, landing, or any bumps along the way.

From these travels, Greg had experience with people's responses to Mitch as well. "Everyone at the airstrips naturally wondered what was in the kennel with all the 'DO NOT TOUCH' signs on it,' he told me. "When I said an eagle, everyone would always double check and ask, 'Do you mean a beagle, like the dog?' And I would say 'No. An eagle.' As a result, I told the story of Mitch no less than a hundred times."

Most people thought it was pretty cool, and wished him luck. Only rarely would someone ask why he didn't just kill it. "For those people, I didn't try to explain," he said. "I probably couldn't do a good job of explaining. It just felt like the right thing to do, even if it was an ass-pain." Another example of Greg's talent for understatement, though I think Dr. Cooper's point about the risk Greg and Scott took every time they had to bring Mitch off base was probably more accurate.

One of the final ass-pains for me was finding transport for Mitch from Virginia to the New York State quarantine site. An Internet search led me to a group that offered rescue animal transport by van, and for a while I thought they would be my go-to guys. However, after some delay while we figured out specific times and locations, they told me they charged fifteen hundred dollars for their services. I swallowed hard, and tried Plan B.

That one entailed my husband and I renting a van and driving to Virginia to pick Mitch up, and bringing him to New York. That seemed like the most direct approach, and the one that gave us the greatest control in case of delays or problems. However, when I e-mailed Dr. Cooper about this, my suggestion was greeted with a rather frantic message saying, basically, no, no, no. You can't drive him. His transport has to be from bonded brokers.

When I told my husband this news he blinked at me and said, "Well, we're broke. Does that count?"

"Also in bondage to an eagle," I replied. "But I don't think it'll fly. So to speak."

Just like Mitch, it didn't. As time ran down toward our ETA, I went in search of the still-elusive Plan C. For a day or so, I floundered my way around the Internet, seeking animal rescue organizations, calling the Humane Society and even the USO. I tried veteran groups, and charitable groups, and more. At first, the only response I got was a kind of head-scratching, followed by "Not sure what to do about that."

But one thing I'd learned was that if you stumble around long enough, in enough different places, odds are sooner or later you'll fall flat on your face into what you're looking for. In this case, that was Pilots N Paws. This group of pilots was joined together into a loosely knit network by Debi Boies, who discovered the need for animal rescue transport through personal experience.

An animal lover and a dog lover, she had done Doberman rescue for a number of years, and four years ago, when it came time for her to add another Dobie to her own household, she decided to adopt a rescue. She found one in Florida, and as she was trying to figure out transport from there to her home, her friend Jon Wehrenberg said he could just fly his small plane down and get him. Sure, Debi said. That's great!

When he returned he asked if she thought there was a need for more of this kind of work—pilots who would transport animals where they needed to go. Debi's response: "You have no idea."

When she inquired with rescue groups about this, the response was immediate. "One e-mail to rescue groups, and it was like the shot heard around the world," she said. "Then we had to get the pilots. That took more time, but as John knew, pilots love to fly and are always looking for a reason to do so. Our pitch to them was, 'Make a Flight. Save a Life.' It didn't take much for them to sign on once they got the word."

A seed was planted. A question was asked and answered, and they went forward. "It just takes the willingness of one person to get things started," Debi said, "and you find along the way there's lots of good people willing to stand beside you."

Yes. I had found that out myself.

The organization is set up as a website where people can put out a call to all pilots who are part of the organization, letting them know what they need. The pilots can then choose their assignment, based on their availability. Though some of the pilots are retired, many are just everyday working people who do what they can. And what they can do is quite a lot.

After the BP oil spill, 58 of their pilots transported 171 dogs to new homes. They've also flown falcons, military working dogs, therapy dogs, potbellied pigs, planeloads of bunnies, and more. Every year they try to run a large "awareness" event, such as the Pilots N Paws Memorial Rescue Flights for the Chesterfield 22. in memory of twenty-two dogs who were taken out and shot by Chesterfield County Animal Shelter workers. It's a small, country shelter, run by the sheriff's department, that was using the dogs brought to them as target practice. Though the case was still under investigation as I wrote this, as Debi pointed out, "the dogs clearly didn't shoot themselves."

Debi believes firmly that the plight of such animals, and the need of other animals, is a human responsibility. "If we don't do it, who will? These animals didn't ask to be mistreated. Humans did that. So we have to clean it up."

Could I have found a better group to work with? Not at all.

By the time I found the Pilots N Paws website I was getting close to deadline, with Greg and Mitch's flight tentatively scheduled for early October, though we didn't yet have an exact date. I posted a notice on the site—"Eagle Mitch needs transport from Virginia to New York"— gave some details, and waited. But not for long.

Within a day I got notice: "Hello, Bchepaitis. Your topic has received a reply since your last visit to Pilots N Paws." In fact, it got quite a few responses, but the one that seemed most feasible was from a New Jersey–based pilot named Jerry Sica, born and bred in Brooklyn, New York.

Little did he know what he was letting himself in for.

CHAPTER 16

We Will Get This Bird Home

Hi All,

I'm sorry I have to write this again. There has been another postponement. The aircraft that is going to take Mitch
home has broken down and is waiting for the part to be
mailed to it so it can continue its journey. I do not have new
details at this time, but tentatively it will be Friday the 8th.
As soon as I have something solid, I'll get it to y'all.

Greg Wright

Jerry Sica and Pilots N Paws turned out to be My Heroes in more
ways than I can count.

When I spoke with Jerry on the phone, his Brooklynese was
homey and reassuring. Here was someone who combined the best of
the eagle and the serpent: down to earth, practical as salt, and ideal-
istic as you would expect from someone who volunteered his flight
time to save animals.

"Jerry," I told him, "the problem right now is that we're on military time. The flight's scheduled, but we won't know until maybe a
day or two before if it'll really take off then." I had already spoken
with Debi about that, and she assured me that her pilots would do

what they could, but Jerry has a job, and while he could be flexible, if the flight changed at the last minute he might be faced with work obligations he couldn't get out of. I also felt like I was asking a lot of him, because the military flight schedule might mean he would have to fly through much of the night himself.

"Don't worry," he told me. "We'll get this done, one way or another. I know other pilots if something goes wrong on my end."

I tried to take deep breaths and relax. Mostly I was unsuccessful. Then, another issue reared its bureaucratic head. When I e-mailed Dr. Cooper and told her about Pilots N Paws, I had to confess I didn't know if they were "bonded and brokered," because I didn't know what that actually meant.

She sighed. Deeply. "We'll have to have a meeting about it here," she said. "And we'll have to talk to the pilot."

I called Jerry again, and let him know. "Jerry," I said, "The USDA wants to talk to you."

"Holy shit," he said. "What did I do wrong?"

"Nothing yet. They're just making sure you're okay, I guess. They want to know about your plane, your flying experience. If you're a serial killer or anything. You know."

"Damn. Should I put on a tie?"

"You got one? They want to talk to you now."

"Holy shit," he said again. "You think I'll do okay?"

"I'm guessing you'll manage," I said.

He did, and the USDA approved Pilots N Paws for Mitch's transport, though he later told Debi it surprised the hell out of him.

However, we were not home yet. Not by a long shot. The days that followed were my idea of hell. We got final word that Greg's flight was scheduled to arrive in Norfolk on October third, at daybreak, and we kept our fingers crossed for good weather because a bad storm front could waylay Jerry's small plane in a heartbeat. Fittingly, that coincided with the Feast of St. Francis, a time when Catholics troop their pets into churches to get them blessed. I could only hope that beloved Italian ambassador for the animals would accompany Mitch all the way.

Maybe he did, but we also had another occupant on the flight. A guy named Murphy, whose law ruled all.

The next day we found out the flight was delayed for twenty-four hours. I called Jerry and he rescheduled his work hours and flight plan. The following day we got word that the flight was delayed again, for another twenty-four hours, and now it would arrive around noon instead of daybreak. I called Jerry, who once again rearranged his life to accommodate us. I felt bad for Jerry, and bad for Greg, who surely must be getting impatient by now. I tried to keep my tone upbeat, positive.

"When I see Murphy, I'll have something to say to him," I e-mailed Greg. "I hope you're holding up okay."

He wrote back that he was doing okay and would be glad to get home. His next e-mail wasn't half so cheerful. After they had boarded and were on their way, a mechanical failure stopped them cold. "I want this plane to land in the states ASAP. I was supposed to be at the beach with my dogs and eating sushi today originally!!!"

It was the first time I'd seen anything like frustration from him, and I felt his pain. There's nothing quite like the feeling of thinking you're on your way home, and having your arrival repeatedly blocked. I'd heard from other veterans that some of their greatest tension happens when home is almost in sight. If their patiently nurtured stoicism is going to dissolve, that would be the time. It was the equivalent of Etana clinging to his eagle, no longer able to see where he had come from, and not yet able to see where he was going.

Though my life wasn't at risk, my stoicism wasn't faring very well either. I had to call Jerry one more time on Wednesday, to let him know the current arrival would be Friday morning, October eighth, at four-thirty a.m., which meant he would have to fly through the night. That is, if he could make it.

When he heard the news he groaned. "I can't do it, Barbara," he said. "That's the one I can't do."

He sounded pretty pained about it, and I felt bad for him. He had already expended a lot of effort to make this flight, and I knew how badly he wanted to do it. But I was also tearing at my own hair, not sure what options were left.

"Oh, God," I groaned in return. "What should I do?"

"Listen, don't panic. I told you, I've got some buddies on stand-by. One of us will get back to you."

"Jerry," I squeaked, "we're running out of time."

"Don't you worry," he said, in the most reassuring Brooklynese I had ever heard. "We will get this bird home."

And that's when Jerry became one of My Truest Heroes. Any old Hero will take on the job when they know they can get it done, and have the fun of completing it, the thrill of being in the action. A Real Hero will take it on when they know the action will go to someone else, but the job still has to be done.

While I paced, fielded some pretty frantic e-mails from the USDA wanting to know the flight plans, and asked St. Francis why he was letting Murphy take over his job, Jerry started making calls. My own phone kept ringing all day—calls from news people who wanted to keep up with the stories, last-minute interviews with journalists, and last-minute calls from the USDA and Fish and Wildlife confirming paperwork and transport routes were all part of that very long day. At four o'clock that afternoon someone from Fish and Wildlife had called to ask who was paying the fees.

"Fees?" I said, gulping. "What fees?"

"Import fees," they said.

"But this is a rescue," I insisted one more time.

The voice on the other end said, "We consider it an import."

I began to bluster, to argue, and the Fish and Wildlife representative cut in. "If it's an import," he said, "sometimes it's also a Military Mascot. For mascots, the fees are waived."

"Oh," I said, getting it. "It's an import. A mascot import."

At nine-thirty p.m. my phone rang again, and I fully expected it would either be another excited reporter or an irritated USDA official reminding me that I hadn't told them anything except that a Pilots N Paws plane would be at the airport in the morning. Instead, the voice on the other end was calm, smooth, and had a mild southern twang.

"Barbara Che—Che—," he said.

"Chepaitis," I confirmed. "Yes, this is Barbara."

"Hi. I'm John Williams, with Pilots N Paws. I understand you have an eagle that needs a ride."

John, a retired lawyer living in Virginia, gave up the first days of his planned motorcycle vacation, grabbed fellow pilot C. M. Funk, and showed up before dawn at the airport to fly Mitch from Virginia to New York. Yet another Hero for the list. This one probably saved my sanity as well as Mitch's life.

The rest of my night involved more calls letting the USDA know what was going on, getting John in touch with them, fielding what I had to field as it came up. I knew I had to be up early to make the drive to the airport in Westchester County where Mitch would land, but sleep was more slippery than an eel that night.

At four-thirty on Friday morning I was up and dressed, imagining the dark at Norfolk's airfield, imagining Greg and other young men in uniform carrying a crate full of eagle out of a military plane. I went to the phone in my kitchen and called the cell phone number I had for Dr. Karen Floyd, who was taking care of Mitch's inspection on entry into the United States.

The kitchen was dark and quiet, and there was something quiet living inside my soul. When I heard a voice on the other end, I spoke.

"Dr. Floyd?" I asked. "Did they make it?"

"Barbara? Yes they did," she replied, sounding calm, as if she did this every day.

"John Williams got there?"

"He did. We're all here, safe and sound."

I let go of a long breath I'd been holding in for some months now. "Is Greg there?" I asked.

"He is. Right here."

Unexpectedly, my throat tightened up. I hadn't let myself realize that I was waiting as hard for Greg to get home safe as I was for Mitch. That was too much to think about. "Can I talk to him?" I asked.

She put him on the phone, and I heard another calm voice. "Hi, Barbara," he said. "How are you?"

"Greg? It's really you?"

"Yeah. I'm home."

"I'm so glad," I said. "I won't keep you. I just—I wanted to hear your voice. I never heard it before."

He laughed softly. "Yeah. It's been lots of e-mails and nothing else, right?"

"It has," I agreed. "Okay. Go get your dogs. Go eat some sushi. Go get some sleep."

"I think I will," he said. "Hey—thank you. Thank you for everything you did."

"Actually," I said, "thank you. *Very* much."

CHAPTER 17

Thirty Days in the Hole

From: Dr. Cooper
To: Everyone
Subject: Eagle Mitch Quarantine

. . . Dr. Floyd or Greg should contact Dr. Davis to alert him to the approximate time the flight should arrive at his Center. Please remember to seal his carrier. The pilot will fly Mitch directly to the quarantine center to be met by either Dr. Davis or Arthur Schwartzberg.

Ms. Chepaitis will be allowed to see Mitch before he enters the quarantine. . . . I think this does it. . . .

When I left my house to go meet Mitch for the first time, the sky was dark and full of stars. By the time I got to the Berkshire Spur it was getting rosy, and mist curled over the land, illuminated and pearly in the dawn. A good day.

I gave myself plenty of time for the drive, not wanting to get lost and arrive too late. As a result, I ended up arriving well before Mitch at the small aviation terminal in Newburgh. This terminal, for small planes and noncommercial flights, was more like a clubhouse than an airport, with comfortable couches and chairs, and cookies and muffins out with the coffee. A few men and women worked behind the reception desk and in back offices, but it was pretty quiet. After I called home to let Steve know I had arrived, and to make sure nothing horrible had happened in my absence, I asked the woman at the reception desk if she could tell me anything about John Williams's flight, due to arrive this morning.

"Is that the one with the eagle? I heard something about an eagle coming in today," she said.

I explained about Eagle Mitch, how he had been saved in Afghanistan and how we fought to get him here. "Oh my God, that's wonderful!" she said. She called another woman over. "Joan, you hear this? You gotta hear this story."

I told it again, and got more of the same. "That's so beautiful," other people said. Then, "Do you need anything? While you're waiting?"

"Just more coffee," I said.

The people at the terminal let me know when the flight was coming in, and told me I could go out on the back porch and watch it land. "Don't go past the porch until the plane's down," they warned me. I had no intention of doing so. But I stood on the porch in the relative quiet of an unbusy terminal, and heard the unmistakable whir of the airplane as it approached, watched with a feeling of unreality as it touched down.

Really? Eagle Mitch would be in that plane? Alive?

Over the past few months both Mitch and Greg had assumed the contours of imaginary friends, fictional friends. Beings I knew only via my computer. Seeing the plane come in was as strange as if a Muppet or a Smurf had suddenly climbed out of the television and sat down at my kitchen table.

But the plane did touch down, and I ran out to it as John and C. M. emerged. I saw the crate, just a regular dog crate that said "Afghanistan Eagle Mitch" on it, and I could hear something moving inside it. It was covered with cardboard, but the first thing I did, before I shook John's hand and before he was out of the plane, was move the cardboard just enough to peek inside. I had to make sure I wasn't imagining things.

From inside the crate a large raptor stared at me fiercely, not at all worried, confused, or afraid. If anything, he was truculent, as if he wanted to know why dinner was delayed.

"Mitch," I whispered. "It's you."

He flapped at me, and stared some more. I smiled back. "You're a very handsome bird," I told him, which was unnecessary. Clearly, he already knew that.

Okay. So it was real. I remembered my courtesy and introduced myself to John and C. M., shook their hands and thanked them heartily. They brought the crate inside, and Dr. Kenneth Davis, from the USDA, arrived. He was charged with the care of Mitch during his U.S. quarantine, and when I shook his hand I felt a little like a mother bringing her child to kindergarten for the first time. When my son was little, I knew how important it was to meet the teacher, make sure she knew you were an involved kind of parent. I felt the same with Mitch.

"Dr. Davis," I said, smiling at him with my best "I mean this" face, "You'll take good care of Mitch, won't you?"

He recognized a nervous parent when he saw one. "I most certainly will," he said. "And you can call me anytime you want an update."

I laughed. "I wonder how many times you'll regret saying that," I said.

He shrugged, and laughed with me. I talked with John and C. M., who were like Jerry, saying they just wanted to help, and were glad to do so. We watched Mitch get loaded into the USDA van. We all went our separate ways.

The ride home was filled with light. Sunlight, after days of rain. The light of leaves turning gold and orange and brilliant yellow. The lightness of flight, possible only when you've hollowed out your bones through hard and good work.

The next thirty days were the quietest I had known in some time. I e-mailed Greg to see how he was doing, and found out he was indeed eating sushi and running on the beaches of Virginia with his dogs.

The thought of that spread warmth through me like my grandmother's chicken soup.

"If all goes well, I'll drive Mitch from his quarantine to Berkshire Bird Paradise in early November. Is there anything I should know about transporting him?" I asked him.

He wrote back, "I would bring a couple of garbage bags to line the floor where his crate is in case of an accident. Once I was taking him to see Major Jenkins and I was sitting outside waiting for the plane to land, and he just blasted the door of the kennel from his rear end. I think he was specifically aiming for the door just to let me know he didn't like the sound of the helicopters in the background. Seriously."

I believed him.

Periodically I checked in with Dr. Davis, who told me Mitch was doing well. Periodically I spoke with Pete Dubacher, who was getting Mitch's aviary ready. Periodically I spoke with reporters who wanted to be at the sanctuary when Mitch arrived.

Once he came out of his U.S. quarantine the USDA would sign off on him for good. I needed no bonded or brokered help to bring him to Berkshire Bird Paradise. I just had to rent an SUV big enough to hold his crate, and get something to line the bottom of it, in case he decided to demonstrate his bad mood through his bowels. He would be leaving quarantine just before Veteran's Day, so there was a good amount of news interest in his story. A friend of mine, a marvelous publicist named Sherri Rosen, sent out a bunch of e-mails to national news stations to see if any of them wanted to cover it. Fox News was interested, and I thought it was a tribute to the spread of Mitch's wings that he could get interest both from Fox and Rachel Maddow.

At Fox, they wanted to know if we could bring Mitch to the station for their *Fox & Friends* show on Veterans Day. Pete was game for it, but at the last minute Fox changed their minds. They had Dolly Parton's eagles scheduled that day, and they thought that would be just too much.

Okay, I thought. So what if celebrity conquers all? I had met some real heroes. I knew they existed, no matter how wicked the world became.

When I posted a Facebook update on Eagle Mitch, praising John and C. M, and Debi, the president of Pilots N Paws, Nick O'Connell, responded briefly: Pilots N Paws was proud to play a part in the life of a lonely eagle. And lots of other people, some old friends and some new, offered congratulations, a big "hoo-ya" for all concerned.

I no longer wondered why this story touched people. The compassion we give to animals heals some of the most wounded places in our souls. That healing then goes out to heal others, in ways large and small.

Later that year my brother, a Franciscan priest, told me about a mass he said for third graders, where he asked them to give their petitions to God. "Pray for those hurt in the tsunami in Japan, and for my sick hamster," one boy offered.

That's worth a giggle, for sure, but it also reminded him that children understand world catastrophes by relating them to their own lives. The compassion a child feels for a hamster is translated to compassion for larger matters. That's how we learn to love.

I had also learned something Navy SEALs get trained to know. A team of people can perform tasks impossible for one person to accomplish. Our success depends entirely on what we can do together.

However, the final leg of the journey was still ahead of me. And for that, I would be driving Mitch to his new home quite on my own.

CHAPTER 18

Asking Toward the Light

I arise facing East.
I am asking toward the light.
I am asking that the day shall be beautiful with light.
I am asking that the place where my feet stand shall be light,
and as far as I can see I shall follow it aright.
I am asking for the courage to go forward through the shadows.
I am asking toward the light.
I am asking toward the light.

Libana

On November eighth, the day Mitch got out of quarantine, I woke up extra early. I had rented my SUV the night before and it was sitting in the driveway, plastic drop cloths in the back portion in case Mitch decided to express his feelings again. I'd spent much of the week coordinating schedules with Dr. Davis in Newburgh, with Pete Dubacher, with a variety of reporters, and with two priests.

That's right. Two priests.

One of them, Father Kevin Mackin, Franciscan president of Mount St. Mary College, would meet me in the USDA parking lot to bless Eagle Mitch as he left the facility. The other, my brother Peter, would meet me at Berkshire Bird Paradise to bless him again when he arrived. There would be a lot of press there, from TV and newspapers, and Anya Tucker and her cameraman from WTEN News would meet me at the USDA and trail me throughout the journey, so I put my face on as carefully as I could at five a.m. on a cold and rainy day.

My husband would stay home, fielding any last-minute calls and managing whatever logistics might come up, then go out to the bird sanctuary to help Pete set up for the reporters and Mitch. I would pick Mitch up and drive him to his new home on my own. Everyone who knew the story was pretty excited about it, and I was getting lots of encouragement online. I was feeling about two parts excitement and three parts frank terror. This was the last leg, the place where I could almost see home-free, but didn't know if I would actually get there.

Have I mentioned that no bird rescue I've ever attempted has been successful? That birds seemed to find me only because they needed a place to die, and I was their pick for that thankless task? And given the way things had gone throughout, I don't think I was being irrational if I anticipated that something would go horribly wrong.

Though I'd had a month of quiet, as I drove to Newburgh that morning I felt every old demon in my soul roaring out something unpleasant. Errant images of car accidents, nuclear explosions, eagles that escaped their crate and flew into traffic, flitted in and out of my mind. One of the disadvantages of being a writer is a vivid imagination. There was not a bad scenario you can come up with that I couldn't do one worse.

When I got to the USDA facilities I was greeted by Anya and her cameraman, and by Father Mackin and his office's PR person. I smiled at them all, gave a few brief words to reporters, and went inside the USDA building to retrieve a bird.

I told the receptionist what I was there for and she directed me to a waiting area. She had a kind face, and her voice was rich and deep as she said, "I think what those young men did was wonderful. I thank them, and I thank you."

It was a real moment in a mostly surreal morning. I appreciated it considerably. A USDA doctor met me in the waiting area. I signed papers (of course), and was told things I hardly heard and can't remember now. All of Mitch's files belonged to me now, including his USDA papers, his veterinarian reports, and his X-rays. It was a fairly thick folder.

I thanked the doctor for caring for Mitch. "You'll miss me here, won't you?" I asked, and he laughed. Then two young men came out of a back room, carrying a crate that said "Afghanistan Eagle Mitch." As we walked into the lobby, I felt motion behind and around me. I turned and looked. Everyone present stood and saluted Eagle Mitch.

When the crate was safely ensconced in the back of the SUV, Father Mackin cracked it open just enough for a little holy access, but not enough so Mitch could get out. The reporters gathered around to take pictures and get film. Mitch glared at them all, daring them to get too close, and when the blessing began he started flapping his wings wildly and sticking his face out, looking fierce. I had a moment when I was worried that his head would start spinning around backward and he would throw up something vile. Or worse, he would express himself as he had with Greg. I was relieved when he seemed to decide that all these people weren't worth fighting with, and he moved to the back of his crate and waited for them to go away.

Reporters took more pictures and asked me questions. They wanted to know how I felt. So did I.

When most of the press and priests were gone, I went back to Mitch's crate and took another peek inside. I wanted a quiet moment with him.

He was agitated at my intrusion at first, but when I began speaking to him softly he quieted and only stared at me with something like curiosity.

And here's the thing about raptors: They don't look at you. They look into you. Through you, to all the places you long to go. Though intellectually I knew Mitch was probably checking out the prospect for food, seeing if I had any or if I *was* food, he gave the impression he was reading my soul, and considering what he'd learned.

"Oh. It's just you again," he seemed to say. "And will you get me where I need to go?"

"I hope so," I muttered at him.

A few more reporters appeared and asked a few more questions. I answered as best I could, smiled as hard as I knew how, got in my SUV, and started driving.

The cameraman from WTEN News rode with me, and after we did a brief in-car interview we just chatted as I drove along, talking easily about birds, about living in the country versus the city, about this and that. It would take about three hours to get to the sanctuary, and I was glad for the company.

"Could you just peek back and make sure he's okay?" I asked him now and then. "He's really quiet."

The cameraman would turn and lift the cover slightly from the crate, and I would hear a scuffling. Then I would breathe again. Mitch was still alive.

My confidence was increasing, or at least my neuroses were subsiding, until we were about forty-five minutes into the drive. Then I noticed a car off the road ahead of us. And another. And another.

"Huh," I said. "What's going on?"

"I'm not sure. Maybe some kind of accident?"

A car ahead of us began a slippy-slidey dance across the road. "Holy shit," the cameraman said. "The road's all ice."

Right.

Of course it was.

At some point as we drove north, the rain had turned to ice. Doubly glad for Father Mackin's blessing, I put my hands hard on the wheel and drove slowly ahead.

At one point we came to a complete stop because a tractor trailer had jackknifed and was stuck. We made our way around it, only to see a car just ahead smashed into the guardrail.

"Just go slow," the cameraman said, talking me through the worst of it. "You can do this. Just don't panic, and stay slow."

He didn't realize that my karma was riding with me as I imagined skidding out, rolling over, Mitch's neck broken in the process. I don't think my knuckles have ever been quite so white. The road got worse as we drove north, the icy rain becoming plain sleet, and then snow. It started falling hard as we approached our destination, accumulating inches as we went. When we got off the interstate near Troy I stopped at a gas station to fill up, and Anya pulled in behind me.

"Quite a day," she said. "Any idea how it'll be at the sanctuary?"

"Bad," I said. That was my best guess.

The cameraman went back to Anya's car to ride with her, and they drove ahead. Now it was just me and Mitch. If anything went wrong, it would be on my watch alone.

Before I got back in the SUV I called my husband, who was already out at Berkshire Bird Paradise. "How's the road out there?" I asked. The final lap to the sanctuary is rugged even in good weather, an unpaved, twisty downhill country dirt road.

"Pretty bad," he admitted. Since he's willing to drive through just about anything, that was saying a lot. "You'll want to go nice and slow," he added.

It was to his credit as a husband that he didn't ask me if I thought I could do it, a mark of his trust in me. "Okay," I said, setting my will and my knuckles. "You think any press'll show up in this storm?"

"Oh, yeah," he said. "They've already been calling to say they're on their way."

"Really?" I asked, surprised.

"You bet."

"Tell them I'm on the way," I said. I closed the phone, got back in the SUV, and crawled along.

In the back of the SUV, Mitch was quiet. In the front, I was terrified. Staying on the road was a challenge as we drove the roads ahead. Look at where you want to go, I kept telling myself. Don't look at the wrecks, or possible wrecks. Stay on your driving line.

By the time we go to the turnoff for the sanctuary road I no longer had any feeling whatsoever in my hands, or in my heart. I took one good skid on the turn, managed to straighten it out without doing any damage, and kept moving forward. The back of the SUV was so quiet I was convinced Mitch had died of a heart attack, picking up on my fear. I took the last mile of the downhill road as carefully as possible, and only skidded three or four times.

Turning into the driveway for the sanctuary was both the best and worst moment: the best because at least I got there, and I hadn't flipped the car over, and the worst because Mitch's crate was still quiet, and now it had to be opened. I imagined our local news that night carrying stories of the eagle that almost made it, showing images of a dead bird in a dog crate from Afghanistan. I felt the weight of every dead bird I had ever held in my hands.

As I got out of the SUV I saw my husband walking down the drive toward me, and just seeing his face made me feel better. He exudes a sense of safety. As he said to me long ago when I had to follow him in my car to a place I had never been before, "When I lead, nobody gets lost."

I walked up to him and let him hug me good. Then we went to the back of the SUV and opened it up. The covered crate inside was still quiet. When Steve's hand moved to take the cover off, I stopped it.

"I don't know if he's okay," I said, my voice a few octaves higher than usual. "He hasn't made any sound. I don't—I'm a little . . ." My words trailed off to silence.

Steve looked at me like I was a little nuts, and removed my hand from his. Without hesitation, he pulled the cover off the crate.

Immediately, I heard Mitch hopping about inside, agitated, protecting his territory. My heart began to beat again. I found a smile that I actually meant.

Alive. Mitch was alive. Still alive.

Steve put a hand on my shoulder. "Okay?" he asked.

"Okay," I replied. "Way okay."

Pete appeared right after that, and he and Steve got Mitch's crate into a wheelbarrow and pushed it through the snow toward his new aviary. I was floaty, as if I had suddenly entered an emotional no-gravity zone. For the first time in my life, a bird I'd helped rescue hadn't died on me. That was a big karma shift, and I was feeling it.

"Wait til you see what I set up for him, Barbara," Pete said as we walked toward the aviary. "I think he's gonna like his new home." I had no doubt. In that I was as secure as if I had brought a puppy to Cesar Millan, the Dog Whisperer. Mitch was now in the hands of the Bird Whisperer.

When we entered the warm, dimly lit aviary, I also knew he was home. This sanctuary, though humble in many ways, has a sense of the sacred about it. A sense of magic. In some ways, it reminded me of the second nursing home we brought my mother to, where the facilities weren't shiny and new but the caring always was. I smelled new hay, laid on the ground to make it soft for Mitch's feet. I heard the soft sounds of nearby pigeons and geese.

The aviary itself was one of the large Quonset hut–like buildings Pete had created to house his many avian residents. The large space was separated into compartments by netting that differentiated spaces for the birds. It was large enough for Mitch to hop around and flap without hurting himself, and it had plenty of tree branches for perches, and a place to hide as well. It was perfect, and it held me the way I'd held hope cupped in my hands throughout this long journey.

Press had already arrived, but they were quiet, influenced by the feel of the place. As Pete brought the crate to the entrance of what would be Mitch's area he talked to them, explaining what he was doing.

"See, I'll just get the crate inside and open it, then Mitch can hop out on his own, find his way around," he said. "He'll feel more secure that way. And I've got him in with Helga—my blind Bald Eagle. She's real placid, so he'll have company, but he won't feel threatened at all."

Pete's actions followed his words. He brought the crate into the netted area where Helga stood quietly dreaming her eagle dreams, opened it, and moved away so Mitch wouldn't feel crowded.

Mitch hopped out right away and stared hard at Helga. She didn't move at all. Mitch flapped his wings at her, turned, and made a dash away from her, going all the way to the other end of his area, where he was stopped by more netting.

Pete, watching, said, "Huh."

"What's that mean, Pete?" I asked.

He pointed to where Mitch was standing, flapping his wings against the netting that blocked him from an area where another eagle lived. "Eddie's in there," he said.

That would be Eddie, the Bald Eagle from Buffalo I had told Greg about, who was shot in the wing by someone who wanted to sell his feathers. On the other side, Eddie was staring at Mitch.

"I think he wants to be with Eddie," Pete said. He went into the closed-off area and opened the netting between the two, and Eddie hopped right over onto Mitch's side. Right away, Mitch cozied up to him, opening his wings and stretching them, opening his mouth the way a juvenile bird will to its parents so it can be fed. Eddie cozied right back. Apparently, they were sympatico, two gunshot survivors who had something to say to each other.

There are many reasons why he may have preferred Eddie to Helga. Maybe he wanted a more vigorous companion than Helga. Maybe he wanted a male companion. Whatever the reason for his choice, what was astonishing to me was the clarity of it. We don't necessarily imagine birds have a preference in these things. We don't think of them as capable of making that kind of choice. And we're wrong. For whatever reason, Mitch clearly wanted to be with Eddie that day. Pete saw that and let it happen without question. Which is why I wanted Mitch with Pete in the first place.

Mitch settled his feathers, and he and Eddie perched together as if they had known each other since the beginning of time. Reporters started asking questions. My brother Peter showed up and blessed Mitch again, but this time Mitch was calm throughout, content with his new home.

What a bird. What a day. What a place. What a strange and joyous life.

Epilogue

Winter came on fast after that day in November, bringing with it an intense season of ice storms, snowstorms, more ice storms. I spoke with Eileen and Scott and Greg, all back in the United States now. When I spoke with Scott his wife had just had their first child, a little girl, and they were moving to Wyoming where he had a job lined up in a coal mine. I didn't like the idea of him having to take that kind of work, but soon after he started his own business and was busy and happy with family and work.

When I spoke to Greg he had just gotten married and was still enjoying his time in Virginia with his dogs and his friends. He strikes me as the kind of person who's good at appreciating happiness, and I hoped that meant plenty of it would come his way.

Eileen continued with her army service, but now she did so here, with her husband.

Because of the bad weather I didn't get out to Berkshire Bird Paradise again until the spring, and the first bird I went to see was Mitch, living in his roomy summer aviary, decorated with a Navy SEAL flag to honor his valiant rescuers. Pete had already told me that lots of people visited the sanctuary because they'd heard Mitch's story. One of those visitors was another SEAL stationed where Mitch was, who said they all got a lot out of having him around, and he was really glad a good home had been found for him.

I walked up to Mitch's aviary and pressed my face against the netting. Inside I could see the tree branches and ropes Pete always puts inside the large aviaries to make the raptors feel at home. There were plants there, too, and places for him to hide if he wanted, lots of room for him to strut his stuff on a floor of earth and leaves that wouldn't hurt his feet. The aviary was high enough for him to hop and flap up onto his perches, and there was water for him to take his baths, along with the remnants of a ratsicle, yesterday's supper.

It was a fine home for a veteran of a foreign war. A well-deserved haven for a bird who carried us all so far.

Mitch, on one of his perches, reacted to the presence of a human, spreading his wings, flapping them, and running toward the netting as if daring me to disturb his new digs. His eyes were full of challenge, letting me know this was his territory and he was ready to defend it. The last time I saw him he still had some abrasions and cuts from his closer quarantine quarters, and his feathers were ruffled, sticking out in places. Now he had no wounds, and he was sleek and shiny and bright, as if someone had just polished him.

"Hey Mitch," I said softly. "You are one handsome fellow. Brave and strong and true. And you look like you still know it." At the sound of my voice he stopped flapping and stared at me in a different way. I kept speaking. "Really handsome," I said again. "You're as healthy as Greg and Eileen and Scott would want. And I'm so damn glad to see you here."

He moved closer to me, and I wondered if he remembered my voice, talking him through our long and snowy ride. Greg told me Mitch would always calm down when he heard his voice. He's a smart bird. I wouldn't be surprised if he was smart enough to recognize an old friend.

After a while, he moved back to his perch, cuddling up to his new aviary mate, Thor, a Golden Eagle who was injured when he ran into a power line. Soon they were joined by Buddy, a rescued hawk.

After a while I left Mitch to his friends and went around the rest of the sanctuary, once again admiring the work Pete does, and what it brings to the world. I have this theory—one of many—that the yearning to protect what's wild and free is a way of preserving what's wild and free in ourselves. I also believe that impulse is one of the best aspects of the American profile. When greed or expediency supersedes that yearning, we've lost a large chunk of what it means to be American. Our American souls are deeply wounded as we witness oil spilling into the Gulf, destroying the land and its creatures. Our American souls rejoice when young servicemen show such admirable compassion for a wounded bird, or when Pete Dubacher takes in another injured hawk or his bald eagles raise another set of chicks to go out into the world.

As I walked to the sanctuary with Pete, he showed me his new wind turbines, part of his plan to make the sanctuary entirely "green." And he showed me a fledgling eagle almost ready for release, brought to him by the New York State Department of Environmental Conservation, which is almost ready for release.

"You want to be here for it?" he asked me.

I'd seen eagles take off from their nests in the wild, and I knew how stunning it could be—the great wings spreading out as the eagle circles, then the pinpoint landing as the bird swoops down for his lunch and flies away again. It makes the air feel cleaner, makes your heart feel as big as the open sky.

Which, in fact, it is. That big. Big enough to save an eagle.

Watching this fledgling take off would mark another high point in my karmic journey with birds: the first time I witnessed a rescued bird take flight.

"I'd love to," I said. It felt like an appropriate reward for helping to rescue Eagle Mitch.

Recently a journalist who was writing a story about Mitch e-mailed me and asked if I could sum up the most important discovery I'd made during those rather extraordinary 137 days. I threw my hands up in the air. I had to write a whole book to do that, and she was asking for a few sentences? But I needed to give her an answer, and the first thing that came to mind was the quote at the beginning of this book:

Love feels no burden, thinks nothing of trouble, attempts what is above its strength, pleads no excuse of impossibility; for it thinks all things lawful for itself, and all things possible.

The hazards of writing make it necessary for writers to understand this. But understanding and feeling are different. We carry some knowledge for years in our heads, and then one day it bursts into flower inside us, a luminous, living thing that invades our hearts as well. That happened for me because of Eagle Mitch. This war-wounded bird took the notion of love and made it dance around.

As much as we carried Mitch, he also carried us, teaching us that the smallest, most humble love can generate something much greater because love is an an energy that grows as it's fed. He taught us that personal power resides not in strength or worldly clout, but in our capacity for love, which can move even the mountains of bureaucracy and corporate interests. And if we could do this, what other good might we be able to accomplish? Anything seemed possible.

Maybe what happened with Eagle Mitch was inevitable, written in both my astrological chart and the circumstances of my life at the time. Maybe it was all coincidence, and I have the writer's penchant for shaping meaning out of random events.

However you view it, I know I needed exactly the kind of healing Eagle Mitch offered. I needed to know it was possible to save one bird, get one good deed done. I needed to know that even the largest institutions and corporations were still composed of humans, and that some of them were deeply compassionate, truly wanting to do what love requires.

And here was the biggest surprise for me: what started as one more struggle became, in the end, just another lesson in love.

Just.

As if there's any more important lesson to learn, at any time, in any way.

Right?

Oh yes. Absolutely right at last.

Author's Note

The SEALs are protective of their own, and rightly so. Therefore, the name of the SEAL involved in this mission has been changed.

If you want to learn more about Berkshire Bird Paradise, their website is http://www.birdparadise.org. I encourage you to visit it, or to visit Berkshire Bird Paradise on Facebook, and to contribute generously to Mitch's ratsicle fund.

And if you need animal transport, or if you're a pilot who wants to make a flight and save a life, please visit the Pilots N Paws website here: http://pilotsnpaws.org.

The quote from Joy Harjo's poem and many other works of wonder can be found in her book of poetry, *The Woman Who Fell from the Sky* (Norton, 1994).

Infinite thanks are due to my husband, Steve Sawicki, who had to put up with me while he was trying to find a job and I was trying to rescue an eagle.

All happiness be yours, darling. There's not another like you in the world.